Learning Korean

Learning Korean

—

Recipes for
Home Cooking

Peter Serpico with Drew Lazor

Photography by Neal Santos

W. W. NORTON & COMPANY
Independent Publishers Since 1923

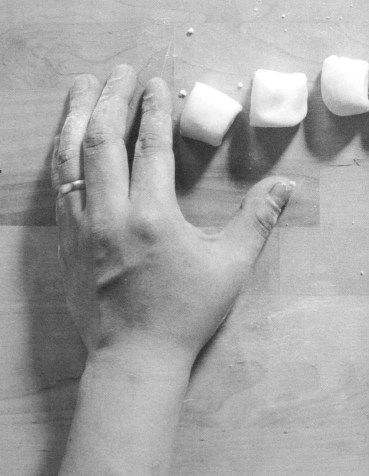

For information about permission to reproduce
selections from this book, write to Permissions,
W. W. Norton & Company, Inc.,
500 Fifth Avenue, New York, NY 10110

For information about special discounts for bulk purchases,
please contact W. W. Norton Special Sales at
specialsales@wwnorton.com or 800-233-4830

Manufacturing by Transcontinental
Book design by Ashley Tucker
Production manager: Anna Oler, Nat Kent

ISBN 978-1-324-00322-9

W. W. Norton & Company, Inc.
500 Fifth Avenue, New York, N.Y. 10110
www.wwnorton.com

W. W. Norton & Company Ltd.
15 Carlisle Street, London W1D 3BS

1 2 3 4 5 6 7 8 9 0

To my mom,
who worked so tirelessly to put a
hot meal on the table every night.

To my dad,
who has always supported me
to live my dreams.

To my wife and best friend,
you make me better every day.

To my daughter,
you are the brightest light.

Contents

· · · · · · · · · ·

Introduction

KOREAN FOOD NOURISHES ME IN A WAY nothing else can—the kind of fulfillment you experience so deeply that using words to describe it seems like a disservice. The easiest and most accurate way to put it is that it just feels right. When I eat Korean food, I feel better.

The give-and-take of salty and sweet. The appealing balance struck among fermented funk, fishiness, and invigorating spice. The wholesome, vegetable-centric approach—"clean" eating, centuries before it was cool. The universe of flavors unlocked atop the building blocks of kimchi and white rice, cornerstones of every meal that partner so well, despite having nothing in common.

I know this is what you'd expect to hear from a Korean person, especially one who works as a chef. But I wasn't always so in tune with my culture, my cuisine, or myself. The truth is, for much of my life, I had no connection to anything Korean whatsoever—originally by circumstance, and eventually by choice.

I've heard many chefs speak of the moments that made them fall in love with food: fond recollections from childhood, cooking side-by-side with parents or grandparents and sharing cherished family recipes. As their careers progress, they expand upon these deeply personal flavors, relying on high-end skills to maximize their impact on diners—maybe creating new memories in the process. Turns out I've taken the exact opposite route. I came up in this industry not knowing a thing about the cuisine running through my veins. Instead, I decided to dive in after experiencing success on a professional level.

Many different factors motivated me, but family is by far the biggest. Cooking is my life's work, yes, but my wife, our daughter, and our loved ones, Korean and otherwise, have all helped me see food for what it should be: not a vehicle for ego, but a selfless expression of generosity and care. It took me years to sort this all out—to work up the knowledge and courage to present a book like this to the world.

/ / / / / / / / / /

My name was Kyung-ho. I was born in 1982, and I ended up at an orphanage in Seoul—not quite as dramatic as being left on a doorstep in the driving rain, but something along those lines.

I first met my parents, Dennis and Sally Serpico, when I was about 2—a doctor's best guess based on the length of my bones, since my birthday wasn't written down anywhere. After several years struggling to conceive, they'd adopted my older twin siblings, Danny and Terra, from Bogotá, Colombia, coming into contact with the orphanage through an organization in Maryland. By the time they wanted to adopt again, the laws in Colombia had changed, so they began looking elsewhere. In 1980s America, it was often easier to adopt from overseas, and South Korea, for many reasons, had one of the most navigable systems of the era.

That is the short version of how Kyung-ho, the Korean orphan, became Peter, the American chef. I don't like to see myself as the beneficiary of arbitrary timing, and I don't want to think of the life I've built as a byproduct of chance. But knowing where I started, and how easily I could have ended up anywhere else but here, has a way of putting things in perspective.

My dad still tells the story about the day they brought me home. *Peter was as neat as a pin. Right off the plane, he went into his room, took out all his clothes, folded them, and put them away in a drawer.* I was already potty-trained, and I had a great appetite. My good habits, apparently, made the 7,000-mile trip with me. My favorite meal was fish and rice, which my mom took pains to prepare for me on top of the food she was cooking for everyone else. To her relief, I adapted quickly. Before long, I was enjoying spaghetti, green peas, and garden salads with ranch dressing, same as everyone else around the table.

Both Chicago natives, Dennis and Sally met as freshmen at the University of Illinois. Mom came from a Polish family, dad from an Italian one. Right out of school, he got a job in the Applied Physics Laboratory of Johns Hopkins University, which is what brought them to the Baltimore area. Dad, an electrical engineer, worked on radar and missiles and other things he still can't really talk about. Mom worked in banking, and later became an ESL teacher. Our parents, the twins, me, and our youngest sister Jackie—we were, and are, your standard-issue American family.

We lived in a nice, unassuming four-bedroom house with a deck and a backyard tire swing in Laurel, about halfway between Baltimore and DC. We went to Hammond High, attended mass at St. John the Evangelist, and rooted for the Washington Redskins. Our parents were both tremendous

athletes—biking, running, racquetball—and encouraged us to be active. When I was 11, we participated in Cycle Across Maryland, a 320-mile ride that took us all over the state on two wheels. I didn't care much for cycling, but I did like baseball. Dad coached me in Little League, and I continued playing through high school, catcher and right field mostly.

On special occasions, we'd go out to a restaurant like The Tomato Palace, which had the red-and-white checkered tablecloths you'd expect to see at a restaurant called The Tomato Palace. But there being six of us, we ate pretty much all of our meals at home. My mom, who passed away in 2004, called all the shots in the kitchen. Dad's domain was the grill, but really he was in charge of dishes.

Mom would have her huge grocery haul from BJ's, then painstakingly plan out everything to portion, store, and freeze, stretching a single shopping trip out weeks. Her Friday night mac and cheese—elbows, extra-sharp cheddar, béchamel—is one meal I remember well. I still make it with my daughter, Charlie, whose favorite part is sprinkling the paprika on top before we

slide it into the oven. Then there was my maternal grandmother's apple pie, always waiting for us when we arrived at her house on Greenleaf Avenue, the best reward after the endless drive to Chicago.

I'd be lying if I claimed I felt mystically drawn to cooking at an early age, the way many chefs are. While I wasn't passionate about it at the time, my high-school jobs did end up being food-related. When I was 14, I ran the snack bar at a swimming pool, but I was let go when I couldn't find anyone to cover my shifts before we left on family vacation. The boss canned me via answering machine, a very '90s way to get fired.

I fared much better at Ledo Pizza, a chain based in Maryland. It started as a part-time summer job, but soon enough—"in typical Peter fashion," as my dad likes to say—I ended up running the place as the assistant manager. The busier it got, the better and faster I performed. I got so much satisfaction from the process—rolling out dough, then topping, baking, and boxing a pie in a blur as I juggled endless orders of wings and sandwiches on the side. Hours would fly by, then I'd suddenly look up and realize, "Oh, I made all that!" I enjoyed it, but it'd be a long time before I realized this was something I'd want to do as a career.

I'm sure this all sounds familiar to anyone who was raised in your typical American suburb—secure, comfortable, and unremarkable, and I mean that in a good way. But I was never a typical American kid.

////////////

On paper, I wasn't different. I took the same classes, played the same sports, ate the same food, watched the same movies, listened to the same music, and worked the same jobs as boys my age. But when you're the lone Asian son of white parents whose other children are Latin and Caucasian (Jackie is my parents' biological daughter), the reality is you stick out, no matter how "normal" you feel.

Howard County is a reasonably diverse place, and I'm privileged to say I didn't experience much discrimination growing up there, beyond a few isolated incidents. My baseball coach referring to me as "Ching Chong" in front of the entire team at practice one day comes to mind. I called him something back, and suffice it to say I never heard that one again. Things were different, though, when we'd visit my grandparents in Chicago. Being young, I didn't pick up on this as sharply as I might now, but my dad says he would always put his guard up when we were out in public together. He knew the judgmental stares from strangers were coming.

I was well into my adult life before I began to grasp how my adoption shaped my views as a person, husband, father, and chef. Growing up, though, the topic didn't come up all that often, and I learned to like it that way.

Over the years, I've discovered that there are certain childhood dynamics common among transracial adoptees. One is the notion that if your immediate family doesn't "see" your race, then it should be a nonissue for everyone else, too. It comes from a place of protection, but it can also breed confusion—as well as you might fit in at home, that contentment doesn't automatically come with you when you walk out the door. The author Nicole Chung, a fellow Korean adoptee, talks about this in her memoir *All You*

Can Ever Know. "Caught between my family's 'colorblind' ideal and the obvious notice of others," she writes, "perhaps it isn't surprising which made me feel safer—which I preferred, and tried to adopt as my own."

While many adoptive parents are hesitant about the topic, afraid of fostering resentment or alienation in their kids, my mom and dad never once tried to downplay that Danny, Terra, and I were not their birth children. On the contrary, they wanted us to embrace our heritage, and got us involved with cultural groups designed to do just that. They also offered to help us find our birth parents, if that's what we wanted.

Of the three of us, Terra was the most curious. As an adult, she actually tracked down her birth mother in Colombia, and she's built a relationship with her, while building a family of her own. Danny, on the other hand, just wasn't interested. And me? It was complicated.

It didn't come up often, but I remember how I felt when it did. My mom would speak in careful hypotheticals. *Maybe, one day, you'll want to go to Korea and find your birth mother,* she'd say, gently opening up the floor for a conversation that I'm sure was as scary for her as it was for me. *No, I won't,* I'd always tell her. After a while, my position firmly established, we stopped talking about it altogether.

It's not that I never thought about it. Of course I wondered who my birth parents were. Of course I wondered about what circumstances led to me being given up—now that I'm a father, the mere thought is too painful to even consider. But in the moment, my parents pushing me to find my Korean identity only reinforced the fact that, in my eyes, it wasn't worth finding. What was the point? Being one of Dennis and Sally

Serpico's kids was all I knew, and as far as I was concerned, that was enough.

Looking back on it, I think I was hesitant because I never wanted it to seem like I was disrespecting my parents by formally acknowledging I was not biologically "theirs." They were always incredibly loving and supportive, and who knows where I'd be without them. Nicole Chung puts it much better in her book: "It would have felt like the greatest of betrayals to tell them I didn't belong in this place, this town, this *life*—all they would hear, I felt sure, was that I didn't think I belonged in our family."

Another common experience among transracial overseas adoptees—this one I could closely relate to—is the anxiety we feel when engaging with our birth culture. When I would interact with Korean people, via those social adoptee gatherings or just in day-to-day life, it always left me feeling like an outsider twice over. Yes, I looked like them. But I didn't speak the language, understand the traditions, or eat the food, so my exposure to this culture—"my" culture, in the most clinical manner—had the opposite of the intended effect.

All this is to say that I've often felt stuck in a holding pattern between two worlds: a birthland I didn't know and a homeland that didn't always seem to know me. Technically, I'm Korean-American. But for the longest time, neither half of that term felt like it fit me.

//////////

Babies for sale. South Koreans make them, Americans buy them.

That jarring headline accompanied a January 1988 article in *The Progressive*, one of many pieces

of its kind published at a time when South Korea was poised to reintroduce itself to the world. That same year, Seoul hosted the Summer Olympics, and the country viewed the Games as an opportunity to showcase its incredible recovery in the decades following the Korean War. But the global media scrutiny also opened many eyes to the country's controversial handling of overseas adoption, at a time when 62 percent of all children adopted internationally were Korean-born.

Though it lasted just three years, from 1950 to 1953, the conflict between North Korea and South Korea devastated the entire peninsula, resulting in unspeakable physical destruction and deaths in the millions. In spirit, South Korea's assertive postwar approach to overseas adoption was benevolent, placing war orphans in stable homes as a wounded country healed. In practice, it was a convenient way to send away babies fathered by foreign soldiers, since mixed-race children were ostracized by society. Over time, though, it grew into something bigger: "the Cadillac of adoption programs," according to *The New York Times*, "because of its efficient system and steady supply of healthy babies"—ethnically Korean babies, like me.

According to South Korea's Ministry of

Health and Welfare, the country averaged fewer than 600 international adoptions annually between 1953 and 1969. In the 1970s, that number rose to 4,600. Through the 1980s—the decade I was born and adopted—the average peaked at nearly 6,600 overseas adoptions per year. Official figures state that more than 160,000 children born in South Korea between the war and the present day were adopted and raised overseas, mostly in the United States. (The unofficial total is likely higher.)

There are many reasons why the Korean adoption system skewed this way. Family bloodlines are valued above all else in the culture, which means single mothers and the "fatherless" children they bear can be shunned by society. And even if a mother wanted to raise a child on her own, she was discouraged by the law. Until 1998, Korean citizenship was conferred solely through the status of the father. If you had no recorded paternity, you weren't a citizen, meaning no access to government services, education, or employment. Children placed in the care of the state, meanwhile, did earn citizenship, which had to have led some mothers to give up their babies against their wishes in an attempt to protect their futures. Additionally, Koreans at large are less comfortable than Americans (like my parents) with the idea of raising a child that is not biologically theirs. NPR has reported that since 1950, only 11 percent of Korean children eligible for adoption have found homes domestically.

Consider these societal factors weighing on a country decimated by violent conflict, and rapidly industrializing in response, and you begin to understand how the climate was perfect for "the Cadillac of adoption programs" to develop. The uncomfortable truth is that more than 50 years of overseas adoptions, encouraged and expedited by those in power, pumped millions of dollars in revenue into an economy struggling to pull itself out of postwar poverty. "It is clear that the government systematically promoted overseas adoption and used children as a tool for economic development while neglecting its duty to protect children's rights," Pastor Kim Do-hyun, director of the nonprofit adoption advocacy group KoRoot, once wrote in *The Korea Times*.

Today, South Korea consistently ranks in the top tier of prosperous countries in terms of GDP, but no substantive changes to adoption policy came about until as recently as 2012, when laws were amended "to reduce the number of Korean children adopted abroad." Things are indeed changing; domestic adoptions have outpaced international cases every year since 2007. But more progressive attitudes can't be retroactively applied to the 160,000-plus Korean-born children whose fates were forever altered by decisions beyond their control.

I know I'm one of the very lucky ones, but I was never able to shake the feeling that there was something missing. It took a while, but food is ultimately what helped me unearth a part of myself I didn't know existed.

////////

Believe it or not, I knew what I wanted to do with my life before I finished high school.

I was an average student—not flunking out, but nowhere close to graduating with honors. Despite the urging from my family and guidance counselors, I had no interest in applying to traditional colleges or universities. The mere thought of four more years sitting in classrooms bored me to tears. I just wanted to work—specifically, I wanted to cook. Even though Ledo's was just a neighborhood pizza shop, my time there convinced me that the kitchen was the right environment for me. I wanted to continue growing the discipline I'd developed there into something greater.

My parents were pleasantly surprised when I told them I wanted to enroll in the two-year culinary program at Baltimore International College. My dad told me it was like someone tossed a switch inside my brain. As a student, I went from extremely uninterested to completely locked in. I think it was as simple as me finally figuring out what I was passionate about. I started classes at 7 in the morning, and afterward I'd head to my line cook job with chef Robert Dunn at Belmont Manor, a historic property in Howard County that hosted weddings, conferences, parties, and the like. The day-to-day cuisine was straightforward stuff, but the one-off wine dinners the Manor hosted every month helped me begin cultivating my creativity.

I credit Rob, my first professional mentor, with kick-starting my career. One day, after I'd finished school but was still working for him, he pulled me aside and basically asked me, "What are you doing?" I don't think I had an answer, but thankfully he had a suggestion teed up. He encouraged me to visit New York City, setting me up with his old sous chef's couch to crash on, plus unpaid stages at Bouley and Lespinasse, two of the top fine-dining restaurants in the country.

I'd never seen anything like it before. I went from this chill, quiet environment where I worked alongside two older guys to these massive, gorgeous, major-league kitchens staffed with 20 maniac cooks who sprinted as hard and fast as they could from the second they clocked in. As a stage, I was only given menial prep work, and I still got my ass handed to me. I loved it.

A week later, I heard from Mike Davis, the chef I had stayed with. His roommate was moving out, and he wanted to know if I was interested in taking the spot. I immediately said yes. It was 2002, I was 19 years old, and I was leaving home—on my own terms, this time. I had absolutely no idea what I was doing. But I felt like I had a chance.

////////

My first paid position in New York was back at Bouley, at the absolute bottom of the food chain. The charitable way to describe the kitchen, and really all kitchens of its caliber back then, is "old-school." The honest way to describe it is brutal. You were given way too much work for any human to complete in the time allotted and zero direction on how to do it correctly, all for basically no money. Then they'd start the timer to see how long it'd take you to quit. Joke was on them—I got fired instead.

I'm glad many chefs industry-wide have stopped romanticizing these unhealthy practices in recent years, realizing how damaging and unproductive they are for everyone involved. I didn't know it then, but it was truly a master class in how *not* to operate my own restaurant. At the time, though, the only thing I knew how to do was push hard.

My next job was with chef Josh DeChellis at Sumile, a French-Japanese restaurant in the West Village owned by the singer Miwa Yoshida. It was much smaller than Bouley but just as intense. Since there were only a few of us in the kitchen, I learned how to do absolutely everything, as opposed to just being tossed to the wolves with no direction. Josh got two stars from the *Times*, so we were doing something right.

In 2004, Miwa sent Josh, my friend and coworker Evan Rich (now the owner of Rich Table in San Francisco), and me to Tokyo to oversee the opening of a new Sumile. It was a surreal experience. *A few years ago, I was stretching dough at a pizzeria in Scaggsville, and now I'm helping a J-pop superstar open a restaurant on the top floor of a luxury building in Shibuya.* Not bad for my first time in Asia, though it was technically my first time back.

I'd go on to work as the executive chef of Jovia on the Upper East Side, plus a few other restaurants, before getting a call from David Chang. Evan and I knew Dave a little from going into the original Momofuku Noodle Bar, where we'd eat ramen, drink beers, and cry about our lives after work. I'd seen a listing he posted on Craigslist, applied, and got a sous chef job working between there and Momofuku Ssäm Bar.

From the very beginning, Dave was thinking expansion. He wanted to grow Momofuku, hard and fast, into a global brand, and he wanted to give sous chefs like me our own restaurants.

To his credit, he accomplished both these goals. He now has holdings in 15 cities across North America. But before all that, when it was just New York, he made me the chef de cuisine, and the part-owner, of Momofuku Ko. It was in this position, the first time I'd ever been fully responsible for our food, our staff, and every other conceivable detail, that I truly started becoming the chef I am today.

I've never been comfortable lingering on past glories, but I'm proud of what we accomplished at Ko—two Michelin Stars, three stars from the *Times*, "Best New Restaurant" from James Beard. *Food & Wine* named me a "Rising Star Chef" in 2009. With the ever-changing tasting menu format, I had complete creative license to experiment with whatever I wanted, and grew so much as a result.

Eventually, I was promoted to Director of Culinary Operations for the entire company, and I was responsible for menu creation and execution at all of Dave's restaurants, from Má Pêche in Midtown to Seiōbo in Sydney, Australia. It prepared me well to open my own restaurant, Serpico, in Philadelphia in 2013. But the biggest reason I look back on my time at Momofuku fondly is that it's how I came to know Julie Choi, who helped me figure out what being Korean means to me.

///////////

People have asked me if my desire to dig up my roots grew out of working with Dave, since he's also Korean-American and there have been some Korean-inspired dishes across the Momofuku menus. The answer is no. The spark came to me in Queens, around a modest table covered end-to-end with the first, and best, *real* Korean food I'd ever tasted.

I met Julie when she was hired as a hostess at Noodle Bar, and someone asked me to train her on the POS system. We got along right away, and she kindly made an exception to her usual policy of not dating people from work. I learned she was a native New Yorker, and that she used to be a buyer in the fashion industry, which explained all the extremely on-trend looks that I, a devoted T-shirt and jeans guy, could not comprehend. I learned that, like me, she was figuring out what she wanted to do with her life, and that led her to restaurants. I also discovered that, while she was Korean-American, our upbringings could not have been more different.

Julie's parents came to America from Korea's southern coast. While she lived as a typical young American woman in Lower Manhattan, back in Queens, she was a traditional Korean daughter. Her dad worked as a carpenter. Her mom, who ran a nail salon with Julie's aunt, still found time to prepare food for the family morning, noon, and night. Instead of mac and cheese, Julie looked forward to sitting down to her favorite soup, whole blue crabs simmered in a spicy anchovy broth, with thick coins of daikon and freshly chopped chrysanthemum (page 100). My food memories tended toward sandwiches and supreme pizzas; Julie's were more panfrying eel and peeling quail eggs.

There is a slight language barrier between Julie's parents and me, but I discovered early on that no extensive dialogue was required for this new chapter of my education to stick. I learned by watching, and of course tasting. I saw how her mom would leave a pot of split pig's feet simmering on the stovetop for days, creating a cloudy

bone broth that was both versatile and elegant (page 79). I witnessed the amount of care that'd go into the marinade for short ribs (page 165), something that's easy to take for granted when you're shoveling down mountains of K-BBQ.

And of course there were the fermentables. Every spring, Julie's mom and aunt would forage ramps from a patch in between their houses and turn it into kimchi that'd stick around through the summer. It was stored, along with dozens of other homemade kimchi, in a separate refrigerator designated solely for this task— a staple of all Korean households, yet one I had no clue about.

Julie and I eventually got married and moved to Philadelphia, and Charlie was born in the spring of 2015. Shortly after, my mother-in-law arranged to come down from Queens and stay with us for a few weeks. While mom and baby were the intended recipients of Halmoni's helping hands, the visit was a gift of a different sort for me. I still remember her pulling up, her car exploding with Korean groceries—it was like she walked into H Mart and told them, "I'll take two of everything." Julie told me this was her own way of saying "I love you," and after she started cooking, I knew exactly what she meant.

Never-ending waves of vegetable banchan, crispy savory pancakes, black bean noodles—every dish my mother-in-law would so effortlessly turn out in our home kitchen was more eye-opening than the last. "Oh, this is just something she'd normally make," Julie would casually observe, every time I raved about how mind-blowingly delicious I found it all.

I'd eaten Korean cuisine before, but it took intimate, substantial moments like these for me to finally get it. Prior to Julie and me dating, I'd more or less given up on finding out how to understand my heritage in a way that made sense to me. I was so focused on my career that I completely missed what is now so obvious. Food was my way in—just not in the way I was accustomed to.

Marrying Julie and becoming part of her family was a sort of immersion therapy, helping me shape my convictions about our cuisine. Here's a big one: There are plenty of excellent Korean restaurants out there, but the best Korean cooking, to me, happens at home. Prior to 2020, I never anticipated that circumstances far beyond my comprehension would force me to examine this belief—and my entire career along with it.

It was clear early on that we'd have to suspend operations at Serpico indefinitely due to the COVID-19 pandemic. We didn't have space for outdoor dining, and the food we were doing just didn't make sense for takeout and delivery. After seven steady years, my staff and I were out of work, just like that. I had some decisions to make. I'd always been reluctant to blend my personal and professional cooking, but these extraordinary circumstances called for new thinking. After talking it over with my partner, Stephen Starr, I landed on a solution: Pete's Place, a pop-up takeout and delivery concept I was proud to describe as "kinda Korean."

The concept—Korean-inflected dishes with wide appeal, designed to travel well—was born of necessity. But I soon discovered that I enjoyed developing these "kinda Korean" recipes as much as the dining public seemed to enjoy eating them. Reverse-engineering everything, from chili glaze chicken wings and pork bibimbap to rotisserie chicken ramen and rice cake fries, to stand up to the rigors of delivery was my kind of creative challenge.

The food sure as hell wasn't traditional, and I caught flack from a handful of purists as a result. But overall it was incredibly well-received. In late 2020, we expanded the pop-up into Washington, DC, for a time, too. Still, walking away from everything we spent nearly a decade building in Philadelphia, and having the pandemic essentially make this decision for us, was tough. But honestly, it was exciting to do something new—especially since it involved (kinda) Korean food.

I'm happy to report that I still feel strongly that home cooks rule when it comes to this cuisine. The recipes you'll find throughout this book lean all the way into the home-cooking spirit. By taking my knowledge and instincts from the restaurant world and applying them to the everyday kitchen, I'm empowering myself, and hopefully others.

//////////

I always found it funny that people assumed my restaurant Serpico was Asian because I happened to be Asian. Sure, we'd play with certain Chinese, Korean, or Japanese ingredients and techniques, but not any more or less than we'd incorporate French, Spanish, or Latin elements onto our menu. Hell, the place was called Serpico and we'd even serve pasta from time to time, but no one ever mistook us for Italian! I bring this up to emphasize a critical point: While this book has my name on the front, it is not a Serpico *Restaurant* book—and it's not a Pete's Place book either.

If you ever see me in a professional kitchen, there's a good chance you will catch me head-down and laser-focused—the kitchen is my comfort zone, where I'm constantly percolating with ideas. I'll be the first to admit that my brain can zig and zag in a million directions when working on new dishes. You might look at an eggplant and see a purple nightshade. I see 30 completely different ways to make it taste amazing—and I'm *always* chasing the perfection that may reside in recipe 31.

At *home*, meanwhile, I'm a completely different cook. Here, I rely on proven, straightforward Korean dishes—recipes I fully trust and vouch for, from start to finish. I believe understanding the difference between these two mindsets is the key to making *everyone* feel comfortable enough to cook. Working in kitchens for so long, I feel that I've proven myself—technique-wise, sure, but also as an effective leader, someone who can connect with every type of learner. This makes me uniquely qualified to present honest and attainable Korean cooking to a mass audience. I know exactly what it feels like to start from scratch, and I'm confident I can lead anyone with an open mind along the best possible path.

The time I spend cooking at home with Julie and Charlie is the biggest inspiration for the recipes that follow. It was important to me to embrace Korean cuisine on my own terms, and I am finally ready to share what I've learned. This is the proud end result of my self-education, informed by years of cooking, eating, reading, travel, conversation, and introspection. It's also a realization of who I am: Korean by heritage and American by upbringing, but a chef and teacher above all else.

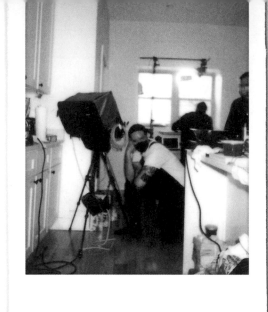

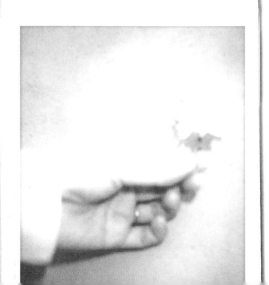

Learning
Korean

Equipment + My Korean Pantry

I SEE THIS NOT AS A COOKBOOK, BUT A cooking book—one specifically designed to be kept within close reach of the kitchen and referenced frequently, as opposed to being a pretty conversation piece stored on a shelf or coffee table. To make the recipes that follow appealing and accessible, I wanted to remove as many barriers as possible for home cooks of all experience levels.

By design, many recipes will augment or complete others, allowing you to tackle a wide variety of dishes without excessive expenditure or waste. I've also opted to use English-language terminology in place of the traditional Korean names of certain ingredients and dishes found throughout this book. This is not an effort to "whitewash" the cuisine for the benefit of unfamiliar readers. It's just the approach that feels most natural and honest given how I grew up. I can't help but view Korean culture through an American lens. By referring to gochujang as chili paste or bibimguksu as Chilled Spicy Noodles (page 124), I'm not disrespecting the Korean identity I'm still learning to embrace but engaging with it in a context that feels authentic to me. Though there are certainly nontraditional techniques and recipes throughout the book, I want to make it clear it's not sanitized or "dumbed down" in any way. It's simply presented with an inclusive readership in mind—a readership that would include me, if I weren't doing the writing.

With this in mind, let's get started with the nuts and bolts. The tools, dishes, ingredients, and pantry staples detailed in this section are what you'll typically find on hand in my home kitchen, which is stocked a little differently than a traditional Korean family's might be (and *definitely* different than a restaurant's kitchen). While there is some stuff that will require a trip to an Asian or Korean-specific supermarket— and the guide below will help you learn what to look for on those shelves—most of it can be purchased at your typical, everyday grocery store.

Equipment-wise, here's what you'll need to cook from this book, beyond a standard stovetop, oven, and grill:

Appliances

- blender
- Instant Pot, pressure cooker, or rice cooker (for Sauna Eggs, page 49)
- stand mixer, with paddle attachment (for Homemade Rice Sticks, page 118) and dough hook attachment (for Knife-Cut Noodles, page 120, and Hand-Pulled Noodles, page 119)

Dishes, Pots, Pans

- 10- to 12-inch cast-iron or nonstick skillet
- heavy lidded oven-safe pot (Dutch oven or cast-iron)
- large oven-safe baking dish
- lidded stock pot
- 10-inch nonstick sauté pan
- small/medium/large lidded pots or saucepans

Tools, Wares

- box grater
- colander
- cutting board
- fine mesh strainer
- metal sheet trays
- metal steamer basket
- small/medium/large metal mixing bowls

Utensils

- all-purpose chef's knife
- dry measuring cups and spoons
- kitchen scissors
- large mixing spoons (metal or wooden)
- liquid measuring cups
- peeler
- potato masher
- spatula
- whisk

Et cetera

- bamboo rolling mat (for Kimbap, page 63)
- glass jars or containers with tight-fitting lids
- latex gloves (for mixing)
- 1-gallon plastic storage bags
- plastic wrap

////////

Many of the ingredients and pantry items detailed below can be found in everyday supermarkets, but some might require a shopping trip to an Asian grocery store, a Korean-specific chain like H Mart, or a visit to an online marketplace.

Daikon radish. One of the most popular radishes used across Asian cuisine, not just Korean, daikon is typically a tall, slender, off-white radish, roughly 8 to 12 inches in length, with a semi-tender flesh and a mild peppery bite. You'll find it incorporated into dishes throughout this book.

Eggs. As much as I would love to cook with nothing but organic and seasonally appropriate vegetables at home 365 days a year, I know this is wildly unrealistic, both economically and from an accessibility standpoint. "Conventional" produce will still yield excellent results. Eggs, however, are an ingredient on which I urge a splurge. The couple extra bucks you'll spend on a top-shelf carton—seek out organic, pasture-raised, and ideally local options—will pay dividends when it comes to results. When you see "eggs" listed among the ingredients in this book, this is what I'm talking about.

Fermented bean paste. Known as doenjang, Korea's versatile flavor base is more aggressive in flavor and coarser in texture (containing partially broken-down soybeans) than fancier Japanese miso. It is typically sold in jars or brown plastic containers in Korean groceries. Available online and on shelves, well-known brands include Chung Jung One, Choripdong, Haechandle, and Haioreum (these names are often printed only in Hangul on packaging). You'll find your favorite via trial and error.

Fish sauce. A vital staple of the Korean pantry, fish sauce (eojang) is one condiment worth investing a little time and attention into. Like commercially available kosher salts (see page 5), fish sauce can fluctuate wildly in flavor and sodium content, which can greatly affect the outcome of a recipe, given its potent concentration. There are many Korean brands, but all the recipes in this book were tested using Red Boat, a high-quality but still relatively affordable Vietnamese brand made using black anchovies. I love using this at home. Remember to store it in the refrigerator after opening.

Glutinous rice flour. This flour is milled from grains of what is commonly known as sticky or sweet white rice. Despite its name, it, like all varieties of rice, does not contain gluten. "Glutinous" instead refers to the naturally sticky consistency caused by high levels of amylopectin, the primary component of starch. This makes glutinous rice flour desirable for sweet dessert preparations, though it has many savory applications, too, like Crispy Rice Cakes (page 113).

Kimchi. The first thing most will picture when hearing "kimchi" is the spicy cabbage-based dish that accompanies every Korean meal. But in reality, the term, which seems to have evolved from "dimchae," an ancient Korean word for salted vegetables, can be used to describe a wide range of dishes preserved through fermentation. We explore a variety of kimchi styles and techniques in this book (see page 9).

Korean chili flake. Known as gochugaru, this ingredient is an absolute must in any Korean pantry. Made from dried and crushed red chili peppers, it has a flavor profile somewhat akin to cayenne, but with deeper smoky heat and a hint of vegetal sweetness. It'll take some experimentation for you to land on the brand you like the best, but as a general rule, the 1-pound, resealable plastic bags found in Asian groceries offer a far better value than anything in a jar or tin.

Korean chili pepper. Known as Cheongyang chili peppers, these dark green chilies are roughly comparable in heat to a jalapeño. There are milder variations on this style that look similar, but you want the slightly spicier ones for recipes that call for fresh Korean chilies.

Korean chili paste. Known as gochujang, this bright red, building-block ingredient is simply doenjang, fermented bean paste, flavored and altered with chili pepper. It is employed throughout the cuisine, and throughout this book, as a flavor base. It is typically sold in jars or red plastic containers in Korean groceries.

Korean chili powder. A finer-milled variation of coarse gochugaru, or Korean chili flake, is used in recipe applications like soups or stews, when you want it to dissolve thoroughly. Find it with all other chili flake varieties and consistencies in the Korean grocery store.

Kosher salt. I use kosher salt over iodized table salt in my cooking because I prefer the flavor and coarser texture. What's extremely important to note here, as weird as this sounds, is that some salts are saltier than others. Every recipe in this book was tested using Diamond Crystal kosher salt, which has 280 milligrams of sodium per ¼ teaspoon serving. That same measurement of Morton kosher salt, meanwhile, features *480 milligrams* of sodium. Every brand is different. While a discrepancy like this won't dramatically alter a stew, it can ruin something like kimchi (page 15), where salt is vital for both seasoning and fermentation.

Maple syrup. I prefer to use classic, widely available maple syrup, as well as honey, in recipes that would otherwise call for granulated white sugar, as it has a lower glycemic index. Controlling the amount of refined sugar in our diets is important for our health, and though this is not some miracle solution, it is an easily executable substitution.

Mirin. Common in Japanese cuisine, mirin is a cooking wine derived from rice that has many applications in flavor-building throughout this book, particularly in marinades. Pure, high-end versions can be pricey, but products sold as "aji-mirin" ("tastes like mirin"), mixed with various adjuncts, are widely available and affordable. You're using mostly small amounts here, so I feel comfortable with this substitution.

Mu radish. Though "mu" technically just means "radish" in Korean, the name most frequently refers to the Korean variety that is plumper and sturdier than daikon, with a distinct green-to-white gradient skin. The flesh is denser and crunchier than daikon, too, which is why I recommend it for longer-lasting kimchi (page 27).

Napa cabbage. By far the most common cabbage in Korean cooking, versatile Napa might also be the most recognizable vegetable in the entire cuisine. Of Chinese origin, this cabbage, typically 2½ to 3 pounds by weight, is identifiable by its football-like shape, dense leaves, and durable ribs. It is the irreplaceable backbone of kimchi and many, many other Korean dishes.

Noodles. Though you'll learn how to make several different types of noodles from scratch in this book, you should also familiarize yourself with styles sold in stores. Glass noodles, also sold as cellophane noodles, are an angel hair–fine translucent variety I use as part of the filling for Pork Dumplings (page 65). Ramyun is simply the Korean version of ramen, sold in dried, quick-cooking bricks (page 102). Made from wheat, elegant and versatile somen noodles are typically sold in pre-portioned bundles (page 125). Korean sweet potato noodles (page 126) have a bouncy, toothy texture, and can sport a purplish color, depending on which type of tuber is used to make them. Typical of Japanese cuisine, udon noodles are the thickest variety in play here, perfect for hearty preparations like Black Bean Noodles (page 122).

Perilla seeds. Though they somewhat resemble sesame, perilla seeds (kkae) are derived from a plant that belongs to the mint family, which explains their slightly medicinal flavor that will appeal to those who enjoy fennel and black peppercorn.

Rice. There are thousands of varieties of rice eaten around the world. Medium-grain white rice is the most popular style among Koreans.

In this book, I suggest using sushi-grade white rice—I just love the quality and consistency you can achieve if you wash and cook it properly—as well as long-grain brown rice, which is not as common with Koreans but wonderful as a healthier option.

Rice flour. Not to be confused with glutinous rice flour, this is simply flour milled from long- or medium-grain white rice. It is used to make slurries for kimchi (page 21), as the base of Korean pancakes (pages 69–73), and many other places.

Rice wine vinegar. "Rice wine vinegar" and "rice vinegar" are the same thing—a condiment made by fermenting the natural sugars of rice into acetic acid, in the same way you'd ferment grapes for red or white wine vinegars. I like that it is more subtle than distilled white vinegar but still has enough of an acidic profile to make an impact in myriad ways.

Seaweed. Commonly sold in thin, dried sheets roughly the size of an 8-by-11-inch sheet of paper, dried, unseasoned seaweed is what to purchase for recipes like Braised Seaweed Salad (page 36). Nori, or laver seaweed, is a more substantial variety you'll use as the outer wrapping for sushi-like Kimbap (page 63). Kombu, or dasima in Korean, is a specific style of dried kelp meant for stocks and broths (page 78) rather than for standalone consumption.

Sesame oil. Use a good-quality toasted sesame oil whenever it's called for throughout these recipes. A little chamgireum goes a long way. Julie and I love to use the 100 percent sesame

HanSang brand at home. For those who don't read Hangul, it's identifiable by its white label, with black writing and a red logo, and a black-and-white bit of paper tied around the cap with twine.

Shiitake mushrooms. Dried shiitake mushrooms are an incredibly useful tool in your pantry, Asian or otherwise. In addition to their extremely long shelf life (store them in an airtight container after you open a sealed package), they provide incredible instant umami to any recipe, and can also be instantly reconstituted in hot water to use as if they were fresh.

Soy sauce. There is massive variety in consistency, viscosity, flavor, and salt content when it comes to soy sauce. There is a specific Korean style called joseon ganjang, for example, with a light color and intense flavor, meant for use as a concentrated seasoning in dishes like soups. For our purposes, though, a standard-sodium brand stocked at your local supermarket or Asian grocery will work well for the recipes in this book.

Sugar. When a recipe calls for sugar, it will either be the conventional, white granulated kind, or raw sugar, which is unrefined and brown in color (not to be confused with brown sugar).

Tofu. Created by curdling soy milk in a process similar to cheese-making, tofu is one of the world's most ancient foods, though it's still a little misunderstood in the United States, even today. Many Americans still see it and use it as a one-to-one substitute for meat, while in Asia it's regarded as a protein all its own. For this book, we'll be using two different textures of tofu, determined by their water content: firm and silken. Firm tofu is usually used for frying, braising, and hearty stews. It is sometimes used for banchan. Silken tofu is the base for soft tofu stew and is occasionally served marinated for banchan.

Kimchi

EVEN IF YOU'VE NEVER HAD KOREAN FOOD, YOU'VE HEARD OF KIM-chi. No single dish is more synonymous with the culture. It's ancient—Koreans have been making it for thousands of years. It's essential—like rice, it's on the table for breakfast, lunch, and dinner. And it's good for you—incorporating fermented dishes into your diet supports healthy digestion and bolsters the immune system, and with kimchi, you're eating your vegetables, too. I've always thought of it as something of a cheat code, instantly balancing and enhancing any meal just by unscrewing a jar.

Nothing has taught me more about Korean cooking, and cooking in general, than kimchi. But as a Korean person who began eating and making kimchi relatively late in life, I understand better than most how daunting it can be. Many uninitiated eaters are wary of its fiery, pungent reputation, and even those who love the stuff can be intimidated by the idea of preparing it themselves. Just keep in mind that the depth of the kimchi category is staggering, encompassing so much more than just spicy, funky cabbage; and making excellent kimchi from scratch, no matter your familiarity with DIY fermentation, is easier than you think. The recipes you'll find in this chapter are designed both to celebrate and democratize kimchi, your gateway into the extraordinary world of Korean food. Though you'll find it incorporated into various dishes throughout the book, kimchi, in all its forms, is the real heart and soul of banchan, the side dishes that accompany a traditional Korean meal.

NOTE: Fermentation is an anaerobic process, which means it does not require the presence of oxygen. Even inside an airtight jar stored in the fridge, your kimchi will continue to ferment, casting off gas that will naturally want to escape. To prevent your kimchi vessel from becoming a pressurized kimchi grenade, make a habit of periodically "burping" your jars or containers if you're not already popping them open daily to enjoy your handiwork.

Countertop Kimchi

1 head Napa cabbage (2½ to 3 pounds), wilted or discolored leaves removed, quartered lengthwise, then chopped crosswise into 1-inch sections

1 medium yellow onion, sliced

1 head garlic, separated into cloves, peeled and thinly sliced

3 tablespoons kosher salt (see Note)

3 tablespoons Korean chili flake

3 tablespoons fish sauce

3 tablespoons maple syrup

1 large or 3 to 4 medium carrots, peeled, halved lengthwise, then thinly sliced into half-moons (about ½ pound)

1 bunch scallions, trimmed and cut into 1-inch pieces (white and light green parts)

2 teaspoons peeled, minced ginger

MAKES ABOUT 1 QUART (16 ¼-CUP SERVINGS)

This recipe is my way of encouraging *everyone*, regardless of familiarity or experience, to make great kimchi at home. You don't need any rare ingredients, special utensils, or expensive equipment. You don't need advanced culinary skills. And maybe most importantly, you don't need a ton of time.

There are hundreds of kinds of kimchi, several of which we'll explore in this chapter. But Countertop Kimchi calls for Napa cabbage, by far the most popular base. Every fall, Korean families get together to prepare huge stores of kimchi to enjoy through the winter, a ritualized tradition known as kimjang. They'll coat head after head of Napa cabbage in their own special marinade. Then it's set aside, and the fermentation—and waiting—begins.

In the old days, they'd stuff kimchi into a clay pot and bury it in the earth; many modern Koreans own separate refrigerators specifically designed to allow the kimchi to ferment in a stable, temperature-controlled environment. All Countertop Kimchi requires, aside from the ingredients, is a couple sheet trays, some heavy books, and a flat surface. In 24 hours, you'll have your very own from-scratch batch of perfectly crunchy, spicy, funky kimchi that will keep for months, and grow even more complex and tasty as time passes. Yes, this process isn't quite as romantic as kimjang, but you probably have stuff to do anyway.

Split the chopped Napa cabbage leaves evenly between two 1-gallon plastic storage bags. Combine all the other ingredients in a large bowl and mix them together thoroughly with a spoon or your latex-gloved hand. Split the contents of the bowl evenly between the storage bags, then use a spoon, tongs, or your latex-gloved hand to ensure the marinade coats the cabbage well.

recipe continues ⟶

Halve Napa cabbage lengthwise, then halve each side, creating four even quarters.

Rough chop cabbage quarters crosswise into 1-inch sections.

Split chopped cabbage evenly between two 1-gallon storage bags.

Split contents of bowl containing all the remaining ingredients between each bag. Use a spoon, tongs, or your hand to mix kimchi thoroughly.

Press out any air and seal the bags. Alternatively, you can also press and seal the bags before mixing...

...and use your hands to massage the marinade into the cabbage until evenly coated.

A Note on Salt for Kimchi

As weird as this sounds, some salts are saltier than others. Every recipe in this book was tested using Diamond Crystal kosher salt, which has 280 milligrams of sodium per ¼ teaspoon serving. That same measurement of Morton kosher salt, meanwhile, features *480 milligrams* of sodium. Every brand is different. While a discrepancy like this won't dramatically alter a stew, it can ruin something like kimchi, where salt is vital for both seasoning and fermentation. The magic number for Countertop Kimchi is 10,800 total milligrams of sodium—that's 3 tablespoons of Diamond Crystal, but only 1 tablespoon plus 2 ¼ teaspoons of Morton. If you're not using Diamond Crystal, which I recommend, make sure to check the label and do the math before making your kimchi.

Squeeze as much air as possible out of the bags before sealing, then place them flat on a metal sheet tray. Cover with a second sheet tray topped with 5 pounds of weight (books work well) and leave it alone on a counter at room temperature for 24 hours. Pressing it this way helps encourage the marinade to spread evenly throughout the contents of the bag.

After 24 hours, the kimchi is ready to eat. It should have a crunchy but not raw texture, an assertive but appetizing aroma, and a well-developed flavor that's balanced between salty, spicy, fishy, and sweet. Refrigerate the kimchi and its liquid in a glass container with a tight-fitting lid. It will keep for up to 1 week, and its flavor will become more complex the older it gets.

Instant Kimchi

Knowing all too well how complex and temperamental the kimchi-making process can be, I took on the challenge of simplifying it for home cooks. Countertop Kimchi (page 13) uses my tried-and-true technique when working with the classic Napa cabbage, but I also wanted to develop an easy "master" method that could be applied to *any* vegetable, regardless of its texture, density, surface area, or water content.

Easier said than done, but after years of tinkering and trial-and-error, I've developed this reliable two-step process, which starts with brining and ends with the introduction of a pre-mixed base packed with flavor. These are static

steps that provide you, reader and fellow kimchi fan, with a controlled launch point.

As mentioned in the pantry section (page 5) and Countertop Kimchi recipe (page 13), different types of salts have different sodium levels and varying levels of coarseness. This can lead to all sorts of problems when making kimchi, but my Master Brine, which jumpstarts the fermentation process in your vegetables, is designed to eliminate any guesswork. (See Master Kimchi Brine, page 20, for a full description of the ingredients and technique. "Master Brine" is used as a shorthand from here forward.) Nothing more than water and salt, it's flexible enough to work with dense

radishes or carrots, as well as delicate watercress or parsley. The only variable you'll be adjusting is the time you allow it to sit, maxing out at 24 hours.

Post-brine, my Master Kimchi Base is a time-saving shortcut that doesn't cut corners when it comes to flavor. (See Master Kimchi Base, page 21, for a full description of the ingredients and technique. "Master Base" is used as a shorthand from here forward.) Think of it as something of a turbo-charged salad dressing, one that will keep improving the quality of your kimchi as it grows more complex and flavorful in the refrigerator. On the pages that follow, I've provided some guidelines for what I like to call "Instant Kimchi." I've chosen herbs and produce that are generally available in any supermarket; some require the Master Brine, while others don't. I encourage you to experiment with ingredients beyond those discussed here. If the results aren't to your liking, don't worry—just purée what you have, and use it as the base for a dressing, a soup, or as a kickstarter for your next kimchi adventure.

Apple Kimchi

Peel 3 Fuji apples, then cut them into 1½-inch cubes. Place in a lidded container and cover with ½ cup Master Base (no Master Brine needed here). Best eaten immediately, but it can keep in the fridge for 2 days.

Bok Choy Kimchi

Cut the dried ends from 1 pound of bok choy, then slice in half lengthwise, or into quarters if it's particularly large. Blanch the sliced bok choy in boiling water for 30 seconds, then immediately rinse under cold water to stop the cooking process. After draining well, place in a lidded container and add 1 cup Master Base (more to cover, if necessary; no Master Brine needed here). Eat within 2 weeks.

Carrot Kimchi

Scrub about 3 medium carrots well with a coarse sponge or scouring pad (no need to peel if you've scrubbed well). Slice as thinly as you can into coins, discarding greens and tops. Master Brine for 24 hours. Drain, rinse thoroughly, then place the carrots in a lidded container and cover with ¾ cup Master Base. Eat within 1 week.

Brussels Sprouts Kimchi

Cut the roots from 1 pound Brussels sprouts, halve them, then slice each half into thin slivers, à la coleslaw. Blanch the slivers in boiling water for 10 to 15 seconds, then immediately rinse under cold water to stop the cooking process. After draining well, place in a lidded container and add 1 cup Master Base (more to cover, if necessary; no Master Brine needed here). Eat within 2 weeks.

Celery Kimchi

Rinse 4 stalks of celery, scrub them well using a coarse sponge or scouring pad, then slice them into bite-size pieces. Master Brine for 24 hours. Rinse thoroughly, then place the celery in a lidded container and cover with ¾ cup Master Base. Eat within 1 week.

Watercress Kimchi

Wash the watercress well, then Master Brine for 12 hours. Rinse thoroughly, then transfer the watercress to a lidded container and cover with ¾ cup Master Base. Eat within 3 days.

Curly Parsley Kimchi

Wash 1 bunch of curly parsley well, blanch in boiling water for 30 seconds, then immediately run the parsley under cold water to stop the cooking process. After it's drained thoroughly, pick the leaves from the stems, then slice the stripped stems into 2-inch pieces, leaving the leaves as-is. Place everything in a lidded container and cover with ¾ cup Master Base (no Master Brine needed here). Eat within 1 week.

Iceberg Lettuce Kimchi

Remove the bottom root from ½ a head of iceberg lettuce. Cut the hard white base portion of the lettuce away from the leaves and slice it as thinly as you can, then cut the remaining leaves into bite-size pieces, roughly 2 inches by 2 inches. Dress everything with 1 cup Master Base (no Master Brine needed here). Best eaten immediately, but it can keep in the fridge in a lidded container for 3 days.

Potato Kimchi

Peel a 1-pound Russet potato, then cut it into 1½-inch cubes. Place potatoes in a small pot, cover with cold water, and simmer them on medium heat for 15 minutes. Pour off the hot water, then cover with cold water until the potatoes are chilled. Drain well, then transfer potatoes to a lidded container and cover with 1 cup Master Base (no Master Brine needed here). Lasts up to 5 days.

Scallion Kimchi

Trim the roots from 3 bunches of scallions, then cut the white and light green parts into 2-inch pieces. Rinse well under cold water, drain, then Master Brine for 24 hours. Rinse and drain the scallions again, place in a lidded container and add enought Master Base to cover. Eat within 2 weeks.

Red Ball Radish Kimchi

Remove the greens from 1 bunch of red radishes, then cut them into bite-size pieces. Master Brine for 3 to 4 hours. Rinse thoroughly, transfer radishes to a lidded container, and cover with ½ cup Master Base. Eat within 5 days.

NOTE: The recipes in this chapter, and most all found in this book, are engineered with my daughter, Charlie, in mind. She's an excellent eater, but is still a little too young to enjoy the levels of salt, heat, or umami that Julie and I are accustomed to. Every kid (and every adult) has different tastes, of course, but as a general rule, there's wiggle room to scale *up* your spice and seasonings from the starting points I provide, as opposed to tweaking in the opposite direction.

Master Kimchi Brine

8 cups filtered water

¼ cup kosher salt

1 pound Napa cabbage (about 6 to 8 leaves), chopped OR

1 to 2 medium Mu radishes, peeled and diced into 1-inch cubes (about 2 pounds)

This master method is the time-saving first step for Vegan Kimchi (page 22), White Kimchi (page 26), and Mu Radish Kimchi (page 27), as well as several varieties of Instant Kimchi (page 16). Letting your vegetables sit in this simple brine ensures a nice baseline of flavor, in addition to jumpstarting fermentation. It's much faster and far less tedious than salting individual leaves of cabbage by hand, which is called for in many traditional kimchi recipes.

I encourage you to use this same water-to-salt ratio and brining method to prepare *any* ingredient to be kimchi'd, paired with my Master Kimchi Base (page 21). See my suggestions on pages 18–19; note that some vegetables will require shorter brining times than the 24 hours I suggest for Napa cabbage and Mu radish below, depending on their weight, surface area, and density. You can also brine a combined batch of Napa cabbage and Mu radish at the same time; just make sure everything is completely submerged in the liquid.

Combine the water and salt in a large bowl or container and stir them together until the salt dissolves. Add the prepared vegetables to the solution, ensuring they are completely submerged, and allow to brine at room temperature, covered loosely with a cloth or paper towel, for 24 hours. The next day, drain the vegetables into a colander or strainer and rinse them thoroughly three to four times with cold, clean water. With the cabbage, squeeze the leaves out between each rinse so they don't become waterlogged before making kimchi.

Master Kimchi Base

2 tablespoons rice flour

½ cup water

1½ cups filtered water

4 garlic cloves, sliced

½ medium yellow onion, finely diced

2 medium carrots, peeled and cut into matchsticks (about ½ cup)

1 teaspoon peeled, chopped ginger

3 scallions, trimmed and thinly sliced (white and light green parts)

2 tablespoons fish sauce

4 tablespoons Korean chili flake

1 tablespoon sugar

MAKES 1 QUART

While it's part of my Pork and Tomato Base (page 80), this magic mixture is mainly designed as a kickstarter for the wide variety of kimchis I hope you make. Apple, bell pepper, carrot, cilantro, onion, ramp, watercress . . . simply brine your vegetables (page 20), add the suggested amount of this base, and boom, instant kimchi. See pages 18–19 for suggestions.

Whisk the rice flour and ½ cup water in a small ceramic or glass mixing bowl and microwave on high for 2 minutes. The heat helps turn it into an even, clingy paste. Combine with all the other ingredients in a 1-quart mason jar. Twist the lid on tightly, shake well to combine, and leave to ferment at room temperature—for 48 hours if you plan on using it immediately, or 24 hours if you want to wait awhile (it will continue developing flavor in the fridge). Store in the refrigerator for up to 3 months.

Vegan Kimchi

1 pound Napa cabbage, chopped and Master Brined (page 20)

1 garlic clove, sliced

½ small yellow onion, sliced

¼ teaspoon peeled, minced ginger

½ medium daikon radish, peeled and cut into matchsticks (about ½ cup)

1 medium carrot, peeled and cut into matchsticks (about ¼ cup)

2 teaspoons Korean chili flake

1 teaspoon maple syrup

SERVES 4 (AS BANCHAN)

Since kimchi so frequently demands some form of fermented seafood (I tend toward fish sauce), plant-based eaters can't always get in on it, so this is a kimchi for them. Look at this recipe as a relatively well-rounded and conservative starting point you should absolutely modify to match your taste. You can easily increase the amount of garlic, ginger, or chili flake if you want bolder flavors, or tweak the onion, radish, and carrot proportions to your liking. Add, edit, and omit until it becomes yours. The purpose of this recipe—and really this book—is not to challenge your feelings about ingredient X and tell you why you're wrong. It's to encourage you to create recipes that will become healthy, reliable, everyday go-tos for you and your family.

Combine all ingredients in a mixing bowl and toss well to combine. Transfer to a glass container with a tight-fitting lid and refrigerate. It will keep for up to 1 month. When eaten immediately, this kimchi as constituted above will be on the milder side since there is no additional salt beyond the brined cabbage, but it will develop more flavor as it sits.

Broccoli Kimchi

1 crown broccoli (about 1 pound) and its stem, cut into bite-size pieces (peel the stem before cutting)

½ medium yellow onion, sliced

5 garlic cloves, sliced

1 medium carrot, peeled and grated

2 teaspoons peeled, minced ginger

1 teaspoon kosher salt

1 tablespoon Korean chili flake

2 teaspoons fish sauce

1/2 teaspoon sugar

SERVES 4 (AS BANCHAN)

What is the most American vegetable? I say broccoli. It's one thing you always can count on seeing at the supermarket, regardless of where you live or the time of year. It's a dinnertime icon, though not always in a good way—it's so universal that it's become a scapegoat for all derided greenery. Regardless of where you stand, there are few vegetables more recognizable. That's why I want to use broccoli to get you into kimchi.

Broccoli florets are a common banchan—blanched, lightly marinated in sesame oil and seasonings, and served at room temperature. I'm a fan of this milder preparation, but I also thought broccoli's familiar texture and flavor would make for a strong foray into at-home kimchi-making. This recipe is easy to execute, with excellent returns—the longer it sits, the better it tastes.

Bring a pot of water to a boil, then carefully add the cut broccoli and stems. Blanch for 15 to 20 seconds, or until it turns a vivid green color, then remove from the pot and immediately run under cold water to stop the cooking process. Combine broccoli, stems, and all other ingredients in a bowl and mix well.

This kimchi can be eaten immediately, but will last covered in the refrigerator for up to a week. If you still have kimchi left after a week, store it in a resealable plastic bag and freeze to add to Kimchi-Pork Soup (page 86).

Cucumber Kimchi

1 seedless English cucumber (about 1 pound), sliced into ¼-inch rounds

2 garlic cloves, sliced

2 scallions, trimmed and cut into 1-inch pieces (white and light green parts)

1 teaspoon kosher salt

1 tablespoon Korean chili flake

1 teaspoon fish sauce

1 tablespoon honey

1 tablespoon soy sauce

2 tablespoons water

SERVES 4 (AS BANCHAN)

It might not jump out at you, but this dish is what made me want to do this book. I remember the first time I tried it: I was in my late teens, enrolled in culinary school in Baltimore, and one of my classmates who also happened to be Korean invited me over for dinner. She casually dished out some banchan her mother had prepared, one of which was cucumber kimchi prepared just like this. Totally elementary to her, but I'd never seen or tasted anything quite like it. I'm not exaggerating when I say it was one of the most delicious things I'd tasted up to that point. So simple, yet so satisfying—spicy, salty, sweet, invigorating. How could something that looked so incredibly simple offer so much big, balanced flavor in each bite? It was one of the earliest times I can remember realizing that Korean food was completely different from anything I'd grown up eating. I like to think this is when I finally started to get it. It's my favorite banchan to this day, but I also eat this as a standalone snack, or as an addition to a salad.

Combine all ingredients in a mixing bowl and toss well to combine. This kimchi can be eaten immediately, but will last covered in the refrigerator for up to a week, becoming more complex the longer it sits.

Tomato Kimchi

1 pint grape tomatoes,
halved lengthwise

1 garlic clove, minced

1 scallion, trimmed and
sliced into thin, wispy ribbons
(white and light green parts)

½ teaspoon peeled, minced
ginger

½ teaspoon kosher salt

1 teaspoon Korean chili flake

½ teaspoon fish sauce

2 teaspoons maple syrup

SERVES 4 (AS BANCHAN)

This dish is not "Korean" in any traditional sense, but it has become
a satisfying go-to when I want to take advantage of the bounty of
tomato season beyond the predictable salt and olive oil treatment.
On its own, it's bright and refreshing when eaten immediately, but
it can easily be repurposed into something new. Use this kimchi
as a taco night topping, fold it into spaghetti with crab, or throw in
some corn to make a summer salad. You can also puree leftovers to a
chunky consistency and eat it like salsa; add cucumbers and jalapeño
for gazpacho. If you have more ripe tomatoes on hand, buzz it all up
together to serve as the base for Baked Eggs (page 61).

Combine all ingredients except the tomatoes in a mixing bowl
and whisk to combine. Add tomatoes and toss until they're well-
coated in the marinade. Serve immediately, or store for 1 to 2 days
in the fridge.

White Kimchi

1 pound Napa cabbage, chopped and Master Brined (page 20)

¼ cup freshly squeezed apple juice (see Headnote)

½ medium daikon radish, peeled and cut into matchsticks (about ½ cup)

1 medium carrot, peeled and cut into matchsticks (about ¼ cup)

2 garlic cloves, chopped

¼ teaspoon peeled, minced ginger

1 scallion, trimmed and sliced into thin, wispy ribbons (white and light green parts)

½ teaspoon fish sauce

SERVES 4 (AS BANCHAN)

Apple juice serves as the catalyst of this kimchi, a cleaner, crisper alternative to those that lead with salt and spice. You can go with store-bought juice if you'd like, or use a juicer, but I'm partial to making my own the old-fashioned way, for a fresher flavor with no added sugar. Over a bowl, work the fruit—two small or one large Gala or Fuji apple should yield what you need—through the coarsest side of a box grater, peel, seeds, stem and all (don't forget to take the sticker off). Then squeeze the grated apple pulp through cheesecloth or a paper towel into a measuring cup. I like cutting the carrots and daikon into a julienne here, to create a textural contrast to my other kimchis in this chapter that call for grating. This recipe can be made vegan by simply omitting the fish sauce, or replacing it with soy sauce.

Combine all ingredients in a mixing bowl and toss well to combine. Transfer to a glass container with a tight-fitting lid. It will keep in the refrigerator for up to 1 month.

Mu Radish Kimchi

½ medium yellow onion

½ small Gala or Fuji apple, peeled and cored

3 tablespoons fish sauce

¼ cup water

1 tablespoon rice flour

2 medium Mu radishes (about 2 pounds), peeled, diced into 1-inch cubes, and Master Brined (page 20)

3 scallions, trimmed and sliced (white and light green parts)

3 garlic cloves, minced

2 teaspoons peeled, minced ginger

¼ cup Korean chili flake

In the wild world of kimchi, radish is the only base ingredient that comes close to rivaling Napa cabbage in terms of ubiquity. Mu radish, which many call Korean radish, is the variety to use here. Plumper and sturdier than the slender daikon, with a distinct green-to-white gradient skin, Mu has the integrity to stand up to kimchi-fication. Given this denser flesh, I like to work a quick slurry of water and rice flour into my mix. In addition to helping the marinade cling to the radishes, this classic trick supercharges the timeline and deepens those tangy, lactic flavors, as rice flour's high starch content is basically an all-you-can-eat buffet for the beneficial bacteria responsible for fermentation.

Puree the onion, apple, and fish sauce in a blender. Bring ¼ cup water to a boil in a small saucepan, then cut the heat and whisk in the rice flour until you achieve a sticky, polenta-like consistency. In a large bowl, combine the brined radish, scallion, garlic, ginger, chili flake, onion-apple puree, and rice flour slurry, and mix thoroughly with a latex-gloved hand. Transfer to a glass container with a tight-fitting lid and let sit at room temperature for 24 hours. The next day, the batch should feature more fiery red liquid than before, thanks to the moisture drawn out overnight. The cubed radishes will have shrunk slightly, and bubbles will have formed as a byproduct of active fermentation (see Note). Move the container to the refrigerator, which slows this process down. It will keep for up to 3 months.

Banchan, Smaller Dishes + Sides

Smaller Dishes + Sides

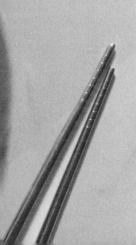

BANCHAN (LITERALLY, "SIDE DISHES") IS THE CATCHALL TERM FOR THE rapturous array of small, snacky preparations—hot, cold, salty, sweet, meaty, fishy, and veggie-based alike—accompanying any Korean meal. Served in a scattering of shallow ramekins comprising a kaleidoscopic variety of colors, textures, and aromas, the banchan course is among the most recognizable visuals of the Korean table, standard both in restaurants, where banchan are usually offered gratis, and in the home. But it's not really a "course" at all, at least in the Western sense.

Though they typically complement what Americans would dub the "entrée," I believe banchan can be the centerpiece of a meal, whether it's a single dish sized up to feed more than one eater, or multiple banchan taken together to create something new.

This chapter features my interpretations of classic banchan preparations, and some nontraditional takes, too. These dishes are accompanied by a collection of recipes that fall somewhere between old-school banchan and American-style starters or appetizers, in terms of portion size and shareability.

Quick-Cured Cucumbers

1 seedless English cucumber (about 1 pound), sliced into ¼-inch rounds

2 teaspoons kosher salt

2 teaspoons cane sugar or raw sugar

SERVES 4 (AS BANCHAN)

While "curing" might evoke thoughts of climate-controlled meat lockers packed with dangling hams, it really just refers to the act of using salt and/or sugar to extract the moisture from a food, manipulating taste and texture in the process. Prosciutto di Parma might take two years, but these cukes will only set you back half an hour. They make for an easy snack, and they're great as a topping for Chilled Spicy Noodles (page 124).

Place cucumbers in a medium bowl, mix in salt and sugar, and let sit at room temperature for 30 minutes. Drain the cucumbers before enjoying. These are best eaten immediately but can be kept in the refrigerator for up to 3 days.

Potato Salad

3 medium russet potatoes (about 1 pound), peeled and cut into medium chunks

1 small Gala or Fuji apple, peeled, cored, and diced small

1 medium carrot, peeled and cut into matchsticks (about ¼ cup)

¾ cup Kewpie mayonnaise

1 teaspoon rice wine vinegar

2 teaspoons raw sugar

2 teaspoons plus ½ teaspoon kosher salt

SERVES 4 (AS BANCHAN)

Gamja saelleodeu, an extremely common banchan at Korean restaurants, appeals to the American palate because it's pretty close to the American-style versions of potato salad you'd find at a summertime barbecue. You're looking for a mashed, almost whipped consistency, and a slightly sweet flavor profile, thanks to the apples, sugar, and Japanese Kewpie mayo, which I like to use here as a binder thanks to its creamier body.

Bring a medium pot of lightly salted water (use ½ teaspoon salt) to a boil, then boil the potatoes for 10 to 15 minutes, until tender. Keep the potatoes in the pot but drain off the water. Mash the potatoes, season them with the remaining 2 teaspoons salt, and let them cool before mixing in the remaining ingredients. Refrigerate in a container with a tight-fitting lid and serve cold. It will keep for up to a week.

Potato Sticks

1 large russet potato (about ¾ pound), peeled

2 teaspoons vegetable oil

½ teaspoon kosher salt

SERVES 4 (AS A BANCHAN)

This banchan is something Julie's mother used to make for her when she was growing up. Unlike the crispy-crunchy packaged snack Americans know as "potato sticks," these are instead steamed to a soft, nearly creamy consistency. Super-simple, but also delicious. Serving this dish at room temperature is key, if you ask me. That's what makes it stand out from American potato-based side dishes traditionally served hot, like mashed potatoes or home fries.

Cut the potato into thin rounds. Place the rounds flat on a cutting board, then slice into small matchsticks. Cover with cold water, rinse, and drain the sliced potato sticks, repeating this process three times to rid them of excess starch. Warm oil in a medium pot or skillet over medium heat, add the potatoes and salt, then cover the pot. Cook for 7 minutes, then remove the pot or skillet from heat. Let the potatoes return to room temperature before transferring them to a serving dish; if you try to move them while they're still hot, they'll break apart. If you're using a skillet, you can also just bring it over to the table to serve after it's cooled.

Potato Pancake

3 medium russet potatoes (about 1 pound), peeled

¼ teaspoon kosher salt

2 tablespoons vegetable oil

Pancake Dipping Sauce (page 73) for serving

SERVES 4 (AS A SNACK)

My mother-in-law also used to make this for my wife, Julie, when she was growing up. Julie has fond memories of dipping the potatoes in the slightly spicy dipping sauce when she was young. It's a very simple and delicious banchan similar to latkes. Crunchy and salty, it can help balance a spice-forward meal, but it can also be enjoyed as you would a McDonald's breakfast hash brown; my daughter loves to dip her bites in ketchup. It's a snap to make on those days you don't have much in the fridge, as you only need three ingredients.

Grate potatoes of the medium holes of a box grater, then rinse the grated potato in a bowl until the water runs completely clear. Drain well in a colander, gently pressing with a spoon or your hand if necessary, and season with the salt. Form the potato into a single, even pancake, about ¼-inch thick. Place the oil in a cold small nonstick pan. The pancake should cover the entire surface of the pan. Place over medium heat and cook for 20 to 30 minutes, pressing occasionally with a spatula to keep the pancake together, until evenly brown and crispy. Flip and cook another 10 minutes, until evenly brown and crispy. Transfer to a paper towel-lined plate to get rid of any excess oil. Cut into eight pieces, like a pizza. Serve with Pancake Dipping Sauce.

Braised Seaweed Salad

4 sheets dried, unflavored seaweed

1 teaspoon soy sauce

1 scallion, trimmed and sliced (white and light green parts)

1 teaspoon water

1 teaspoon maple syrup

1 teaspoon sesame oil

½ teaspoon kosher salt

SERVES 4 (AS BANCHAN)

A banchan classic, salty, savory miyeok muchim pairs well with any other sides from this chapter for a satisfying light lunch, coupled with steamed rice and a fried egg. It's also a zero-waste way to give a second life to the kombu you use to make Anchovy Stock (page 78)—skip over the initial soaking/braising in that case, since you've already done it—but any dried, packaged seaweed (miyeok) will work, so long as it's unflavored.

Place the dried seaweed in a medium pot or saucepan and cover with 2 cups cool water. Soak for 30 minutes, then bring to a boil, reduce heat to low, and simmer for 30 minutes. Meanwhile, place the remaining ingredients in small bowl and whisk to make a dressing. Drain the seaweed, then cut into bite-size pieces. Transfer to a serving bowl and pour the dressing over. This dish is best served and eaten immediately.

Marinated Bean Sprouts

1 teaspoon peeled, minced ginger

1 scallion, trimmed and thinly sliced (white and light green parts)

1 teaspoon kosher salt

1 teaspoon toasted sesame seeds

2 cups mung bean sprouts, rinsed thoroughly

SERVES 4 (AS BANCHAN)

Mung bean sprouts are a healthy and versatile ingredient, as Koreans and many other Asian cooks can attest. They are an excellent vessel for the flavors of ginger and toasted sesame, in particular. This banchan (kongnamul muchim) can work as a fridge snack, as part of a packed lunch, or as a mouth-cooling accompaniment to a spicy entrée at dinnertime. It's also an easy way to extend the lifespan of leftover sprouts, which always seem to go bad quicker than you can eat them.

Bring a medium pot of water to a boil. Meanwhile, combine the ginger, scallion, salt, and sesame seeds in a mixing bowl large enough to eventually hold the sprouts. Add the rinsed sprouts to the boiling water—let them cook for 3 minutes if you like crunchier sprouts, and 5 minutes if you prefer them softer. (Since they are so delicate, you do not have to wait for the water to return to a boil to start your countdown.) Strain the sprouts and immediately run them under cold water—they should look translucent, and be a little flexible without breaking. Add to the mixing bowl, tossing well to incorporate the seasonings. Allow the sprouts to marinate for a minimum of 30 minutes before serving. They can be kept in the refrigerator for up to a week.

Marinated Mushrooms

¼ teaspoon peeled, chopped ginger

1 garlic clove, sliced

2 scallions, trimmed and sliced into thin, wispy ribbons (white and light green parts)

1 tablespoon soy sauce

1 tablespoon maple syrup

1 tablespoon toasted sesame seeds

1 tablespoon sesame oil

One 8-ounce package sliced button mushrooms

SERVES 4 (AS BANCHAN)

Mushrooms are an object of great fascination and adulation in chef circles, as foragers and purveyors are constantly plying us with rare, luxurious, hyper-seasonal varieties to incorporate into our menus. For this recipe, though, the entry-level, pre-sliced buttons you can find in any grocery store are the way to go. Cleaning and processing mushrooms is one of the most tedious kitchen tasks there is, and for people with demanding schedules, kids, or both (aka me), the time saved is huge. It's really all about what you do with them, anyway. This is my take on beoseot muchim, another common banchan; you can easily make this your own by adjusting the ginger, garlic, soy sauce, and maple syrup in the quantities you prefer. Note: This recipe requires marinating overnight, so plan accordingly.

Combine all ingredients except the mushrooms in a bowl and mix well. Toss in the mushrooms, stirring to coat thoroughly in the dressing. Cover and refrigerate overnight to marinate. They can be kept in the refrigerator for up to a week.

Pickled Iceberg Lettuce

½ head iceberg lettuce, core removed, ripped into bite-size pieces

1 garlic clove, sliced

½ teaspoon kosher salt

2 tablespoons rice wine vinegar

2 tablespoons apple cider vinegar

2 tablespoons mirin

2 tablespoons water

2 tablespoons maple syrup

SERVES 4 (AS BANCHAN)

Iceberg lettuce doesn't get much respect. People love to chide it for its lack of nutritional value and taste. While I can't rebut the first point—it is mostly water, after all—I've always found its flavor distinct, and more versatile than we give it credit for. Given how widely available iceberg is, not to mention its remarkable longevity in the crisper, I wanted to come up with a creative and easy way to make it Korean-ish. This pickled preparation is the perfect acidic foil for a rich main, like Braised Pork Belly (page 155) or BBQ Pork Belly (page 154). Enjoy it as a side, use the leaves as an every-bite condiment, or throw some on top of a sandwich the way you would with regular lettuce. I personally like an equal-parts mix of rice wine and apple cider vinegars here. Alone, they can be either too delicate or too aggressive, respectively; combining them nails the balanced vinegar profile I want for this banchan. Note: This recipe requires marinating overnight, so plan accordingly.

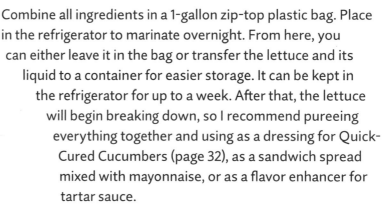

Combine all ingredients in a 1-gallon zip-top plastic bag. Place in the refrigerator to marinate overnight. From here, you can either leave it in the bag or transfer the lettuce and its liquid to a container for easier storage. It can be kept in the refrigerator for up to a week. After that, the lettuce will begin breaking down, so I recommend pureeing everything together and using as a dressing for Quick-Cured Cucumbers (page 32), as a sandwich spread mixed with mayonnaise, or as a flavor enhancer for tartar sauce.

Pickled Daikon Radish

1 medium daikon radish, peeled, then sliced into pencil-size pieces (about 1 pound)

⅓ cup rice wine vinegar

½ cup mirin

2 teaspoons ground turmeric

2 teaspoons kosher salt

SERVES 4 (AS BANCHAN)

Store-bought pickled daikon tends to be very sweet and is packed with preservatives, so I prefer this healthier homemade version, which mellows and deepens in flavor over time. The vibrant yellow color comes from turmeric, which complements daikon's already earthy and slightly pungent qualities (this might be the smelliest recipe in this book, but that's just the way it is). Turmeric has a tendency to stain anything it comes into contact with, so be mindful when handling it. These radishes are also the key ingredient in Kimbap (page 63), Korea's answer to the sushi roll.

Place the daikon in a metal bowl (to avoid turmeric stains) and set aside. In a small saucepan, bring the remaining ingredients to a boil. Remove from heat and allow the liquid to cool to room temperature, then pour over the daikon. Transfer to a lidded glass container (plastic will also stain). You can eat this banchan right away; it will keep in the refrigerator for up to a month.

Scallion Salad

3 scallions, trimmed and sliced into thin, wispy ribbons (white and light green parts)

1 teaspoon Korean chili flake

1 teaspoon soy sauce

SERVES 4 (AS BANCHAN)

A traditional accompaniment for Korean barbecue, this instant salad (pa muchim) also works well as a condiment for rice dishes, like Zucchini Rice Porridge (page 130). To achieve the cut you want here, align the blade of your knife nearly parallel with the scallion vertically, then slice up and down as thinly as you can. Given the interior structure of the scallion, it will create thin, wispy ribbons that will hold the chili-and-soy dressing well.

Put the sliced scallions in a fine mesh strainer, then submerge in ice water for 10 minutes to mellow their pungency. Shake the scallions dry, then toss with the Korean chili flake and soy sauce. Serve immediately.

Marinated Spinach

3 cups frozen spinach

1 garlic clove, minced

1 teaspoon soy sauce

1 teaspoon sesame oil

This is one healthy vegan side I always have on hand in my fridge—eat it for breakfast with rice and a fried egg, use it as banchan, roll it up in Kimbap (page 63), or fold it into Sweet Potato Noodles (page 126). I prefer to use frozen spinach for this dish in lieu of fresh—it keeps things easy by taking the guesswork out of the blanching process.

Bring a medium pot of water to a boil, then add the frozen spinach and boil until thawed, about 1 minute. Drain in a fine mesh strainer and rinse under cold water, then use a spoon to press out any excess water. Transfer to a bowl and add the remaining ingredients. It will keep in the refrigerator for 3 to 4 days.

Marinated Tofu

One 14-ounce package silken tofu

1 scallion, trimmed and thinly sliced (white and light green parts)

3 tablespoons soy sauce

1 tablespoon maple syrup

1 tablespoon rice wine vinegar

¼ teaspoon Korean chili flake

SERVES 4 (AS BANCHAN)

Tofu's texture varies wildly and is based on how long it's pressed before packaging. One way I like to explain it to the unfamiliar is comparing it to cheese: If extra-firm tofu is hard Parmesan, silken tofu would be melty, wobbly burrata. The most common place you'll see silken tofu in Korean cuisine is as the star of bubbling-hot soondubu, a beloved spicy stew where it is accompanied by various meats, seafood, vegetables, and an egg that cooks right in the broth. Here, I'm taking advantage of its tender, creamy texture and the speed with which it absorbs a marinade to prepare a quick and shareable banchan perfect for a dinner party. No need to get fancy when serving it—simply spoon out hunks for everyone and drizzle a bit of the dressing over top.

Drain the tofu and place in a large bowl. In a small bowl, whisk the remaining ingredients to make a dressing, then pour it over the tofu. It can be served this way, at room temperature, immediately, but the longer the tofu sits, whether on the counter or in the fridge, the better-marinated it will become. If you wish to serve it warm, microwave the tofu in 1-minute increments until you reach your desired temperature.

Steamed Eggplant

4 Asian eggplants (about 1½ pounds), cut into 2-inch batons

2 scallions, trimmed and sliced into thin, wispy ribbons (white and light green parts)

¼ cup Korean chili peppers, seeded, sliced very thin

2 garlic cloves, minced

½ teaspoon peeled, minced ginger

2 tablespoons soy sauce

2 tablespoons sesame oil

1 tablespoon maple syrup

1 teaspoon kosher salt

SERVES 4 (AS BANCHAN)

Here is another dish that I love for its flexibility. It's vegan; it can be enjoyed hot, cold, or at room temperature; and it works just as well as a meal for two or banchan for four. I prefer Chinese or Japanese eggplants here. Smaller than the more common Italian eggplant, they have fewer seeds, helping them maintain their shape and texture through steaming, and their flavor is subtle enough to take on a marinade well. Try your best to keep your eggplant cuts as uniform as possible so they steam evenly, and keep a close eye on the process; if they go too long, they'll break down too much to be properly dressed.

Place a steamer basket in a pot over a small measure of water. Arrange the eggplant batons evenly across the steamer basket, turn the heat to high, and cover the pot. While the eggplant is steaming, whisk the remaining ingredients in a bowl.

Check the eggplant after 8 to 10 minutes; when it's done, it should be soft, but not broken down. Careful to keep the pieces intact, immediately transfer the contents of the steamer into the bowl, then gently toss so the hot eggplant absorbs its dressing well. This dish is best served and eaten immediately, but it can be refrigerated in an airtight container for up to 3 days.

Roasted Beech Mushrooms

Two 3.5-ounce packages beech, or Hon-Shimeji, mushrooms

1 tablespoon vegetable oil

1 garlic clove, minced

1 tablespoon soy sauce

1 teaspoon sesame oil

1 teaspoon maple syrup

SERVES 4 (AS BANCHAN)

Beech, or Hon Shimeji, mushrooms are the ones sold in those charming little cartoon clusters, with a bunch of photogenic mini-caps attached to a stump. More affordable than oyster mushrooms and stocked at most grocery stores, these 'shrooms have a bitter aftertaste when eaten raw, but cooking them lightly brings out a subtle, pleasant nuttiness. There's not much to this recipe as I don't want to overpower their natural flavor and texture.

Cut the stumps off the mushroom clusters and freeze to use later for stock. Heat the oil in a skillet over medium heat and cook the mushrooms for about 5 minutes, stirring occasionally, until they get some nice color. Transfer to a mixing bowl, tossing with the garlic, soy sauce, sesame oil, and maple syrup. Serve immediately.

Battered Zucchini

1 large Korean zucchini or
2 American zucchini (about
¾ pound), sliced into
½-inch rounds

1 teaspoon all-purpose flour

1 egg

1 tablespoon fish sauce

1 tablespoon vegetable oil

Pancake Dipping Sauce
(page 73) for serving (optional)

SERVES 4 (AS BANCHAN)

Anyone who grows zucchini, or knows someone who does, is familiar with that certain point in the summer when you're just drowning in them. Since you can only tolerate so many zoodles, here is another easy-to-execute dish for your repertoire. Hobak jeon is a classic warm-weather banchan that fits into any meal, and it's especially good for large groups. The combo of crispy, lightly battered exterior with tender, barely adulterated zucchini flesh never gets old for me. Korean zucchini tend to have a broader circumference than the dark green zukes you typically find in American grocery stores, but there isn't a huge difference in flavor.

In a medium bowl, toss the zucchini and all-purpose flour, ensuring each piece is lightly coated. In a separate bowl, whisk the egg and fish sauce, making sure to break down the egg white, then dip and coat the floured zucchini rounds in this egg batter. In a large skillet or sauté pan, heat the vegetable oil over medium heat. Working in batches to avoid overcrowding, cook the battered zucchini until lightly browned, about 3 minutes per side. Use a spatula to transfer finished zucchini rounds to a wire rack lined with paper towels. Serve as banchan, or with Pancake Dipping Sauce as an appetizer. The zucchini can be enjoyed hot or at room temperature; cooked zucchini pieces can be held inside an oven set to warm.

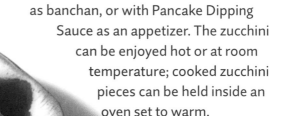

Burdock Root

1 teaspoon vegetable oil

8 ounces fresh burdock root, scrubbed, peeled, and thinly sliced on the bias

2 tablespoons soy sauce

1 tablespoon maple syrup

2 tablespoons water

1 teaspoon sesame oil

1 teaspoon sesame seeds

SERVES 4 (AS BANCHAN)

While burdock may be unfamiliar to many American eaters, it's prevalent throughout East Asia, Korea included. The most commonly consumed part of the burdock plant is its taproot, which resembles horseradish if it were stretched out to the length of a lightsaber. The beige, shoot-like flesh beneath the ruddy skin is the part to eat. Comparable to salsify, parsnip, or carrot in its earthy flavor, raw burdock is extremely tough, but the upside is that it maintains an appealingly chewy, crunchy bite no matter how you cook it. Here, we're basically stir-frying it with simple additions for an easy yet impressive banchan.

Heat the vegetable oil in a large sauté pan or skillet over medium heat. Once the oil is shimmering, add the burdock and cook for 5 minutes, stirring frequently. Add the remaining ingredients and continue stirring until nearly all the liquid has cooked off. Serve warm or cold.

Perfect Soft-Boiled Eggs

SERVES 4 (AS BANCHAN)

A flawless soft-boiled egg, the kind with the soy sauce tint and pretty runny yolk that sits atop your noodles in a ramen shop, is always an impressive feat. It's not difficult to do at home—you just have to be careful and precise. I love to eat these on their own, or with a little steamed rice and kimchi, but they're also the ideal addition to "Instant" Ramyun for One (page 102), Salmon and Kimchi (page 57), or Zucchini Rice Porridge (page 130).

4 eggs

1 teaspoon baking soda

2 tablespoons soy sauce

Start by tempering the eggs, either by letting them sit out for 1 hour or submerging them in a bowl of hot (but not boiling) tap water for 30 minutes. In a medium pot, bring 4 cups water and 1 teaspoon baking soda to a boil. Once the water is boiling, carefully add the eggs to the pot and cook them for exactly 6 minutes. Remove the eggs and run them under cold water to cool. Peel them while they're still slightly warm, submerged in a bowl of water, being careful not to break the whites. Store the eggs with the soy sauce in a 1-gallon zip-top plastic bag or quart container, but prioritize enjoying them as soon as possible—unlike heartier hard-boiled eggs, they only keep in the refrigerator for 2 days.

Perfect Hard-Boiled Eggs

SERVES 4 (AS BANCHAN)

This is my grandmother's tried-and-true method for hard-boiled eggs. She passed it down to my mom, who passed it down to me, and now I'm sharing it with you. It just works, plain and simple. I won't bore you with the science stuff, but the baking soda makes the finished product much easier to peel. In my house, we love hard-boiled eggs for breakfast, lunch, and for quick before- and after-school snacks.

4 eggs

1 teaspoon baking soda

Place the eggs in a medium pot and cover with 4 cups water and 1 teaspoon baking soda. Bring to a boil, then turn off the heat, cover, and let stand for 13 minutes. Remove the eggs and run under cold water to cool. Peel them while they're still warm, submerged in a bowl of cold water. They can be kept in the refrigerator for up to 1 week.

Sauna Eggs

4 eggs

1 teaspoon kosher salt

SERVES 4

A common snack served at Korean spas and bathhouses—per the custom, you crack it open on your head to eat—a sauna egg is distinguished by its soft tan hue and satiny yolk. The "whites" turn brown thanks to pressure-cooking, which triggers a Maillard reaction between the sugars and proteins naturally found in the albumen—the same thing that happens when you sear a steak or bake a loaf of bread. As a result, sauna eggs gain an incredible toasted flavor, like brown butter or roasted chestnuts. I make mine at home the way many Koreans do, inside my pressurized rice cooker, but you can also use a traditional pressure cooker or an Instant Pot.

Start by tempering the eggs, either by letting them sit out for 1 hour or submerging them in a bowl of hot (but not boiling) tap water for 30 minutes. Add the eggs, 2 cups water, and the salt to a rice cooker, pressure cooker, or Instant Pot and cook for 45 minutes, starting the timer once your device has achieved pressure. Let the eggs cool down before enjoying. They can be kept in the refrigerator for up to 1 week.

Rolled Omelette

4 eggs

2 tablespoons Anchovy Stock
(page 78)

2 ribs from small Napa cabbage
leaves (about 1 tablespoon),
finely diced

1 tablespoon yellow onion,
finely diced

1 tablespoon finely diced
peeled carrot

½ teaspoon kosher salt

1 tablespoon vegetable oil

SERVES 4 (AS BANCHAN)

Think of this omelette as the Korean answer to Japan's tamago. Yes, it takes a little practice, but once you master the rolling technique, you'll feel empowered to customize this recipe in any way you like. The most important thing to remember here is that it does not take very much heat, or very much time, to cook eggs well. Using a pan with a lid helps immensely, as it encourages even cooking throughout this multi-step process. Enjoy this omelette on its own as breakfast for two, as banchan alongside soup, or roll it up in Kimbap (page 63).

Combine all ingredients except the oil in a mixing bowl and whisk thoroughly, ensuring the egg whites and yolks are well beaten. In a medium or large nonstick sauté pan, warm the oil over low heat. Pour one-third of the egg mixture into the pan, evenly coating the entire cooking surface, cover, and cook 1 to 2 minutes. Once set, use a spatula to carefully fold one-third of the omelette over onto itself, toward you, then repeat this action twice more—you will have the beginnings of your rolled omelette resting in the portion of the pan closest to you.

Push the omelette back toward the top of the pan. Adding more oil if necessary, pour another third of the egg mixture into the empty space below the first omelette, and again cover the pan until the raw egg solidifies, another 1 to 2 minutes. Carefully repeat the three-step rolling process again—you're now creating additional layers. Slide the omelette toward the top of the pan, then repeat the same steps one last time with the final third of the egg mixture. Allow the omelette to cool completely before slicing it into eight even pieces.

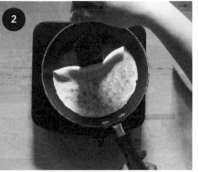

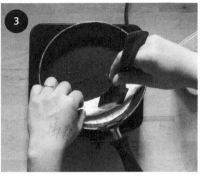

Add one-third of the egg mixture to the pan, being sure to coat the cooking surface evenly.

Cover the pan for 1 to 2 minutes to set the mixture, then use a spatula to carefully fold one-third of the omelette back onto itself.

Repeat this folding motion two more times—your omelette is beginning to take shape.

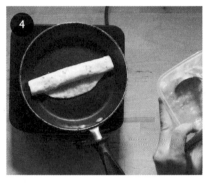

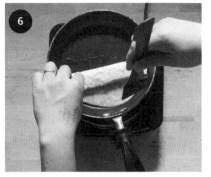

Push the omelette toward the top of the pan.

Add another third of the egg mixture below the omelette, evenly coating the portion of the pan closest to you.

After covering the pan for another 1 to 2 minutes, use a spatula to repeat the three-step rolling process again.

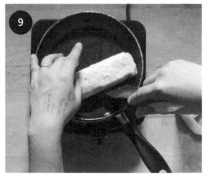

Push the omelette toward the top of the pan, then add the final third of the egg mixture below it.

After covering the pan for 1 to 2 minutes more, give the omelette its last three rolls.

Allow the omelette to cool completely before slicing it.

Rolled Omelette (page 51)

Sweet and Salty Soybeans

½ cup dried black soybeans

2 tablespoons soy sauce

1 tablespoon rice wine vinegar

1 tablespoon raw sugar

2 tablespoons maple syrup

SERVES 4 (AS BANCHAN)

Ingredients derived from soybeans are all over Korean cuisine, from soy sauce and tofu to the fermented pastes that form the backbone of many soups and stews (page 74). With the classic banchan kongjorim, however, the legumes themselves are the star. Subtly sweet and nutty on their own, the dried black soybean, available at any Korean market and in many American groceries, is our starting point. We're not doing much to them aside from working in some additional flavor, both sweet and savory. Given the unique notes at play here, I wouldn't recommend serving this alongside more complex, composed rice or noodle entrées. I personally like it best as part of a banchan-only spread, accompanied by white rice and kimchi, though you may find a different way to love it. This recipe requires an overnight soak, so plan ahead.

Pick through the soybeans and discard any that are broken or discolored, then rinse in a fine mesh strainer under cold water a couple times. Combine the beans and 2 cups of water in a medium pot and let soak overnight, covered, at room temperature. The next day, discard the soaking liquid and replace it with 2 cups fresh water. Bring the pot to a boil, then reduce the heat to medium-high and cook, uncovered, for about 10 minutes, stirring occasionally so the beans don't stick to the bottom of the pot. Stir in the soy sauce, rice wine vinegar, raw sugar, and maple syrup, then drop the heat to medium. Continue cooking, stirring regularly, for another 20 minutes, until the beans are chewy and the liquid has mostly evaporated, save for a few tablespoons. Be mindful of burning toward the end of the process. Serve cold or at room temperature. They can be kept in the refrigerator for up to 1 week.

Smaller Dishes + Sides

Steamed Fish and Kimchi

1 cup Countertop Kimchi (page 13)

Two 5-ounce white fish fillets (black bass, cod, halibut, grouper, monkfish), skin removed

2 scallions, trimmed and sliced into thin, wispy ribbons (white and light green parts)

1 tablespoon peeled, chopped ginger

2 tablespoons sesame oil

1 tablespoon white sesame seeds

Steamed rice and banchan of your choice for serving

SERVES 2

The most important step in this recipe is starting with quality fish that's fresh, not frozen. The cooking is relatively foolproof, so don't concern yourself with what variety you use—it's all about what you like and what's available. The steaming technique I suggest here lessens the chance you'll overcook the fish, a common concern; I also love how the fish flavors the kimchi while the kimchi flavors the fish. If you don't own a steamer or steamer basket insert, you can easily create your own. I place a dolsot, the traditional Korean bowl, in the middle of my Dutch oven to serve as a pedestal for my fish-and-kimchi plate, add water, then cover the whole thing with the lid. Make sure you're using plenty of water, as the cooking time is longer than the typical steam.

Add water to your steamer, making sure it doesn't touch the tray above. On a plate that will fit inside the steamer, make a ring of kimchi, place the fish in the middle, and top the fillets with half the scallions. Cover the plate tightly with plastic wrap, then set it in the steamer, making sure it's not touching the water. Bring the steamer to a boil, lower slightly to a steady simmer, cover, and steam for about 40 minutes, until the kimchi is hot and the fish is cooked through. Carefully remove the plate from the steamer, remove the plastic wrap, and top with chopped ginger and the remaining scallions. In a small pan, heat the sesame oil until smoking, then carefully pour it over the ginger and scallion. Finish with sesame seeds, and serve immediately with steamed rice and banchan.

Salmon and Kimchi

1 cup Countertop Kimchi
(page 13)

1 large Idaho potato (about
¾ pound), peeled and diced
large

½ cup Anchovy Stock
(page 78), chicken stock, or
water

2 scallions, trimmed and
cut into 2-inch pieces
(white and light green parts)

1 teaspoon soy sauce

1 teaspoon mirin

¼ teaspoon peeled, minced
ginger

Two 4-ounce salmon fillets,
skin on

SERVES 2

Mackerel and kimchi is a classic Korean combination, but I've opted here to replace that fish, which some find overpowering, with the more delicate salmon. (Prefer mackerel? Simply swap in fillets of equivalent size.) Using skin-on fillets adds crucial fat and flavor to the dish; it's easy to remove after cooking if you're not into it. The salmon basically quick-steams atop the potato-kimchi stew in its final minutes of cooking. Using chicken stock or water instead of Anchovy Stock (page 78) will dial down the fishiness even more, if that's your preference. Eat this quick sorta-stew with steamed rice and a Perfect Soft-Boiled Egg (page 48).

Combine all ingredients except salmon fillets in a small pot. Cook, covered, over medium-high heat for 10 minutes, or until potatoes are nearly tender when pierced with a fork. Place the salmon fillets on top of the vegetables, cover again, and cook for an additional 5 minutes, until the fish is cooked through.

Fried Fishcakes

8 ounces frozen squid, tentacles and bodies cleaned, bodies sliced

8 ounces shrimp, any size, peeled and deveined

1 small yellow onion, chopped (about ¼ cup)

2 garlic cloves

2 egg whites

1 tablespoon sugar

1 teaspoon kosher salt

½ teaspoon ground white pepper

2 tablespoons all-purpose flour

2 tablespoons cornstarch

2 tablespoons rice flour

½ cup vegetable oil, for frying

SERVES 4

Calling these pan-fried snacks "fishcakes" is a slight misnomer since we're using squid and shrimp, but "Fried Mollusk Crustacean Cakes" just doesn't work. Credit to those crustaceans, in finely blended form, for the smooth, "bouncy" texture I find so appealing here. The banchan equivalent of the coolest kid in school, the fishcake fits in everywhere—bobbing in a brothy soup, folded into fried rice, nestled in greens as part of an at-home ssam (lettuce wrap) dinner. But don't forget to try them on their own—I make these for my daughter's lunch, and she loves using her chopsticks to dunk them in Pancake Dipping Sauce (page 73) or straight soy. I purposely held back on salt in the puree because most frozen squid comes salted, but fry off a single trial-balloon fishcake to begin, eat it, and tweak the remaining puree as you see fit. While we're on the topic: Breaking down the squid's bodies pre-puree is imperative. Squid flesh is so taut and resilient that larger pieces can jam up your blender blades.

Combine the squid, shrimp, onion, garlic, egg whites, sugar, and salt in a blender and puree. Transfer the puree to a large mixing bowl and fold in the white pepper, flour, cornstarch, and rice flour. Heat the vegetable oil in a small nonstick pan over medium heat (you're looking for a temperature of about 325°F). Using a spoon, form a golf ball-sized dollop of the seasoned fishcake batter and drop it into the hot oil. Fry for about 3 minutes a side; you should be able to fit 4 to 5 fishcakes in the hot pan at a time. Rest finished fishcakes on paper towels and repeat the process until all of your batter is cooked. Serve warm.

Bubbling Egg

4 eggs

½ teaspoon fish sauce

1 scallion, trimmed and sliced into thin, wispy ribbons (white and light green parts)

1 cup White Pork Bone Broth (page 79) or chicken stock

¼ teaspoon kosher salt

SERVES 4 (AS BANCHAN)

This is one of those breakfast-in-a-pinch dishes that somehow ends up seeming far more elegant than the process actually entails. I think it has something to do with the airy, delicate, soufflé-like texture the eggs take on—something like a blue-collar Korean version of the fancy Japanese egg custard chawanmushi. Anyway, you don't have to tell anyone how easy it is to do. I like it spooned right out of the pot and onto some steamed rice, with a little kimchi on the side.

Crack eggs into a bowl and whisk them with the fish sauce and scallion greens (reserve the white parts for garnish). Combine the broth or stock and salt in a small saucepan or 6-inch Korean ceramic pot and bring to a simmer over medium heat. Slowly add the egg mixture to the simmering liquid, stirring constantly. Reduce the heat to low, cover, and cook for 5 minutes. Remove the lid, sprinkle the scallion whites on top, return the heat to medium, replace the lid, and cook for 1 additional minute. Serve immediately.

Baked Eggs

4 eggs

1 tablespoon vegetable oil

½ medium yellow onion, sliced

1 red pepper, seeded and chopped into ¼-inch pieces

2 cloves garlic, sliced

1½ cups Pork and Tomato Base (page 80)

½ cup Anchovy Stock (page 78) or chicken stock

SERVES 4

This is a Korean-American cook's take on Eggs in Purgatory or Israeli shakshuka, two savory, slightly spicy breakfasts that I love. This is the perfect place to whip out my Pork and Tomato Base (page 80), which, if you have it at the ready, adds instant flavor without the wait. My wife, daughter, and I love to make this together on weekend mornings, with Braised Seaweed Salad (page 36), toasted bread, and a little Korean Chili Sauce (page 177) on the side.

Crack the eggs into a bowl, being careful not to break the yolks, and set them aside. Add the oil to a shallow sauté pan. Over medium heat, sweat the onion, red pepper, and garlic in the oil until the vegetables start to soften but don't yet begin caramelizing, about 10 minutes. Add Pork and Tomato Base and Anchovy Stock and increase the heat to high until the mixture starts boiling. Gently introduce the cracked eggs, reduce the heat to medium, cover, and cook your eggs how you like them—4 to 5 minutes for runny yolks, and 7 or so minutes if you prefer them cooked through. Serve immediately with any accompaniments you like.

Ground Beef Kimbap

Large sheets of nori or laver seaweed

Easy Stovetop Rice (page 129) plus 1 tablespoon rice wine vinegar and ½ teaspoon kosher salt

Ground Beef Bulgogi (page 159)

Pickled Daikon Radish (page 40)

Marinated Spinach (page 42)

Rolled Omelette (page 50)

2 medium carrots, peeled and cut into matchsticks (about ½ cup)

Sesame oil

SERVES 4

Since it consists of vinegared rice and various fillings rolled up in nori, it's easy to brand Kimbap as Korea's answer to Japanese maki, but at its heart it's a grab-and-go convenience food—closer to a sandwich than sushi. When I make this for my daughter's school lunch (it's great at room temperature), I'll rummage through the fridge in the morning and just wing it. My Kimbap is just as likely to feature turkey breast, cucumbers, and cheddar cheese as anything Korean. The filling suggestions below are just that, but if you're on a tear and experimenting with the preceding banchan recipes, this is an excellent way to make good use of leftovers. Note: You will need a bamboo rolling mat.

Place a sheet of nori or laver seaweed, shiny side down, on top of your bamboo rolling mat. Using your fingers, cover two-thirds of the sheet with a thin, even spreading of slightly warm or room-temperature rice (about ¾ cup), leaving the remaining third furthest from you empty. With a dampened finger, smear a scant layer of rice across the top lip of the seaweed sheet, which will help keep it closed when you roll it up. Arrange whichever toppings you're using in uniform rows, starting about 1 inch from the bottom of the sheet, taking care not to overload it.

Use the bamboo mat to roll the Kimbap up and away from you, over all the fillings; the bottom of the seaweed sheet should land right where the rice ends. Through the mat, firmly push and squeeze down on the Kimbap, ensuring a tight initial roll. Lifting the edge of the bamboo mat hanging over the Kimbap slightly so it doesn't get caught underneath, firmly roll it again to complete the Kimbap.

Rub your knife with sesame oil—you can also use a brush to season the outside of the Kimbap with a light layer of it—before slicing it into 10 to 12 even pieces.

Soy-Braised Beef

8 ounces beef stew meat (preferably chuck), cut into 2-by-2-inch pieces

½ cup soy sauce

¼ cup sugar

5 garlic cloves, sliced

1 teaspoon black pepper or Black Pepper Oil (page 175)

2 Korean chili peppers, cut in half and seeded

2 Perfect Hard-Boiled Eggs (page 48), peeled

SERVES 4

A popular banchan option in Korea, jangjorim is a recipe that my mother-in-law made frequently for Julie when she was growing up. Traditionally served cold but equally good hot, it is a perfect accompaniment to a light soup for lunch or dinner. The beef comes out tender and sweet, with the subtlest bit of spice. Often this dish includes quail eggs, but I chose to go with chicken eggs, as they are more widely available.

Add the beef stew meat to a large pot with enough cold water to cover it. Bring to a boil, maintain the boil for 3 minutes, then dump the water, scrub out the pot, and rinse off the purged beef. This will help remove any funky "barnyard" odors and flavors.

Return the meat to the pot and add the 2½ cups water. Bring back to a boil, reduce heat to low, and simmer for 30 minutes, until the beef is uniformly brown, resembling pot roast. Add the soy sauce, sugar, garlic, black pepper, and Korean chili peppers, and cook for 20 to 30 minutes longer, until the meat is tender.

If you plan to serve the dish hot, add the peeled hard-boiled eggs to the pot for the final 5 minutes of cooking time. If you're planning to eat it cold, add the eggs to the cooking liquid just before removing the pot from heat to slightly "season" them, then refrigerate the beef and eggs together.

Pork Dumplings

1 pound ground pork

1 cup cooked glass noodles, chopped

2 garlic cloves, minced

2 scallions, trimmed and sliced (white and light green parts)

¼ teaspoon ground white pepper

2 tablespoons soy sauce

1 tablespoon sesame oil

36 packaged 3.5-inch dumpling or potsticker wrappers

Canola oil, if pan-frying

MAKES APPROXIMATELY 36 DUMPLINGS

For all their popularity, dumplings can be intimidating to make at home, at least for people who didn't grow up doing it in a traditional Asian household. Thankfully, it's not a difficult process, and the filling and wrapping, the most time-consuming part on paper, is a relaxing activity I love to tackle with my family. This is my personal mandu, a universal pork dumpling that works just as well for entertaining as it does for quick family meals or snacks; they freeze well, and can be pan-fried, steamed, or poached, depending on your preference. The glass noodles in the pork mix might be my favorite part. It's a simple addition that adds so much texturally.

Combine all ingredients except dumpling wrappers in a large bowl and mix well. Cook off a spoonful of the mixture in a pan to check on the seasoning, adjusting the garlic, white pepper, and soy sauce to your taste if necessary. Add 1 level tablespoon of the filling to the center of a dumpling wrapper, lightly wet the edges of the wrapper, then fold the wrapper over and securely pinch it into a half-moon shape. You can separate the wrappers and lay them out individually for a sort of assembly line feel, or just peel them one-by-one from the packaged stack, which I tend to do. Rest completed dumplings on a floured baking pan about 1 inch apart to ensure they don't stick together. Cook the dumplings immediately if you're not freezing them—3 minutes per side over medium heat in a lightly oiled pan, 5 minutes in a steamer, or about 5 minutes in boiling water if you prefer them poached (7 minutes if you're poaching fully frozen dumplings).

To freeze uncooked dumplings, arrange them on a baking pan or plate that fits into your freezer, then freeze for 30 to 45 minutes, until solid, before transferring them to an airtight zip-top plastic storage bag.

recipe continues ⟶

Place a level tablespoon of filling in the center of the dumpling wrapper.

Lightly wet the edges of the dumpling wrapper to help bind it together. Keeping a small dish of water within close reach will expedite this step tremendously.

Fold the filled dumpling wrapper into a half-moon shape, pinching along the dampened edges to seal it securely for cooking or freezing.

Tofu-Mushroom Dumplings

12 baby carrots

1 tablespoon canola oil, plus more if pan-frying

2 garlic cloves, sliced

1 teaspoon peeled, minced ginger

4 large shiitake mushrooms (about 3 ½ ounces, or 1 cup), sliced

2 scallions, trimmed and sliced (white and light green parts)

½ pack firm tofu (7 ounces), cut into ¼-inch cubes

2 teaspoons kosher salt

½ teaspoon red chili flakes

1 tablespoon white sesame seeds

1 tablespoon rice flour

24 vegan dumpling wrappers

MAKES 24 DUMPLINGS

Boiled carrot acts as the all-important binder in this meatless (and vegan) mandu filling for your dumplings, so make sure you mash them well. This will help make sure the filling doesn't turn out crumbly and fall out of the wrappers. As with the pork dumplings, these can be pan-fried, steamed, or poached, and they freeze well.

Slice the baby carrots into ¼-inch coins, then boil them in 4 cups of water for 30 minutes, until thoroughly mushy. Drain, transfer to a large mixing bowl, then mash them as finely as possible. Add canola oil to a large nonstick skillet and place over medium-low heat. Add the garlic, ginger, mushrooms, and scallions, then sauté, stirring occasionally, until most of the liquid is cooked off, about 8 minutes. Transfer contents of the skillet to the mashed carrot bowl, then add the tofu, salt, chili flake, sesame seeds, and rice flour. Mix thoroughly, cover, and refrigerate 1 hour.

Add 1 level tablespoon of the filling to the center of a dumpling wrapper, lightly wet the edges of the wrapper, then fold the wrapper over and securely pinch it into a half-moon shape. You can separate the wrappers and lay them out individually for a sort of assembly line feel, or just peel them one-by-one from the packaged stack, which I tend to do. Rest completed dumplings on a floured baking pan about an inch apart to ensure they don't stick together. Cook the dumplings immediately if you're not freezing them—3 minutes per side over medium heat in a lightly oiled pan, 5 minutes in a steamer, or about 5 minutes in boiling water if you prefer them poached (increase this time to 7 minutes if you're poaching fully frozen dumplings). To freeze uncooked dumplings, arrange them on a baking pan or plate that fits into your freezer, then freeze for 30 to 45 minutes, until solid, before transferring them to an airtight zip-top plastic storage bag.

Onion Pancake

½ cup all-purpose flour

¼ cup rice flour

1 teaspoon kosher salt

1 egg white

½ cup sparkling water

¼ cup chicken stock or water

1 medium yellow onion, thinly sliced

4 scallions, trimmed and sliced into thin, wispy ribbons (white and light green parts)

1 tablespoon Korean chili flake

2 tablespoons vegetable oil

Pancake Dipping Sauce (page 73) for serving

MAKES 2 PANCAKES

If you love buchimgae but aren't too hot on spice, this is the one for you. Traditionally, the onion-based versions of these pancakes are heavy on the scallion (the popular pajeon), but folding thin slices of a conventional yellow onion into the batter really encourages it to caramelize nicely in the pan. This particular recipe can also be easily tweaked into a mixed seafood pancake, probably the most popular variety in Korean restaurants—the crisped-up dough, along with shrimp, scallops, mussels, squid, and the like, is so easy to love (particularly after a few beers). All you need to do is replace the sliced onion with a thawed ½ cup of the same individually quick-frozen seafood mix used to make the Seafood Stew (page 96). You'll find individually quick-frozen (IQF) seafood mixes at most everyday grocery stores and in all Asian supermarkets.

In a large bowl, combine both flours, salt, egg white, sparkling water, and stock/water and whisk well. Fold in the onion, scallion, and chili flake. Heat 1 tablespoon of the oil in a large nonstick skillet over medium heat. Ladle half the batter (just under 1 cup) into the skillet and cook for 5 to 6 minutes until golden brown. Flip the pancake and continue cooking until the second side is golden brown, 5 to 6 minutes more. Repeat with the second tablespoon of oil and remaining batter. The resulting pancakes should be about 7 inches in diameter and ½-inch thick. Slice each pancake into six to eight even pieces and serve with Pancake Dipping Sauce.

Kimchi Pancake

½ cup all-purpose flour

¼ cup rice flour

¼ teaspoon kosher salt

1 egg white

½ cup sparkling water

¼ cup kimchi liquid, chicken stock, or water

1 cup Countertop Kimchi (page 13), drained (reserve liquid) and finely chopped

4 scallions, trimmed and sliced into thin, wispy ribbons (white and light green parts)

1 tablespoon Korean chili flake

2 tablespoons vegetable oil

Pancake Dipping Sauce (page 73) for serving

MAKES 2 PANCAKES

Buchimgae, or Korean pancakes, are at once a traditional snack and a huge crossover hit. Most commonly made with kimchi, mixed seafood, vegetables, or a combination of these folded into the batter, they are standard fare for street vendors, and a legendarily restorative food among drunk Korean revelers. But versions can also be found on the menus of Korean-American restaurants, high-end and casual alike, since it's such a recognizable format—the dough falls somewhere between a crepe and a Chinese-style scallion pancake in consistency.

When I was a kid, my mom would use sparkling water for her homemade waffles, which did wonders lightening up the batter. I've borrowed this trick for this kimchi pancake, my own version of standard kimchi-buchimgae. Blending together all-purpose and rice flours creates a crispy, chewy texture, kept airy by the sparkling water and egg white. This is a useful go-to when you have an insubstantial amount of kimchi left and you need to clear some room for the next batch.

In a large bowl, combine both flours, salt, egg white, sparkling water, and kimchi liquid and whisk well. Fold the Countertop Kimchi, scallion, and chili flake into the batter. Heat 1 tablespoon of the oil in a large nonstick skillet over medium heat. Ladle half the batter (just under 1 cup) into the skillet and cook for 5 to 6 minutes until golden brown. Flip the pancake and continue cooking until the second side is golden brown, 5 to 6 minutes more. Repeat with the remaining tablespoon of oil and second half of the batter. The resulting pancakes should be about 7 inches in diameter and ½-inch thick. Slice each pancake into six to eight even pieces and serve with Pancake Dipping Sauce.

Chrysanthemum Pancake

½ cup all-purpose flour

¼ cup rice flour

1 teaspoon kosher salt

1 egg white

½ cup sparkling water

¼ cup Anchovy Stock
(page 78), chicken stock, or
vegetable stock

2 cups fresh chrysanthemum,
both leaves and stems finely
chopped

1 small zucchini (about
⅓ pound), cut into ½-inch
half-moons

4 scallions, trimmed and
sliced into thin, wispy ribbons
(white and light green parts)

1 tablespoon Korean chili flake

2 tablespoons vegetable oil

Pancake Dipping Sauce
(page 73) for serving

MAKES 2 PANCAKES

My Crab Soup (page 100) calls for fresh chrysanthemum, the greens of the flowering plant that are a classic accompaniment for seafood. Asian markets sell this stuff in big bunches, so it's likely you'll have plenty left over. This pancake is a great way to put it to good use. Both the leaves and stems of fresh chrysanthemum are edible, with a grassy, mildly bitter, herbaceous flavor. Chop them finely here so they meld into the batter evenly.

In a large bowl, combine both flours, salt, egg white, sparkling water and stock/water and whisk well. Fold in the chrysanthemum, zucchini, scallion, and chili flake. Heat 1 tablespoon oil in a large nonstick skillet over medium heat. Ladle half the batter (just under 1 cup) into the skillet and cook for 5 to 6 minutes until golden brown. Flip the pancake and continue cooking until the second side is golden brown, 5 to 6 minutes more. Repeat with the second tablespoon of oil and remaining batter. The resulting pancakes should be about 7 inches in diameter and ½-inch thick. Slice each pancake into six to eight even pieces and serve with Pancake Dipping Sauce.

Pancake Dipping Sauce

2 tablespoons soy sauce

2 tablespoons rice wine vinegar

½ teaspoon maple syrup

¼ teaspoon Korean chili flake

¼ teaspoon sesame seeds

1 scallion, trimmed and thinly sliced (white and light green parts)

MAKES ABOUT ¼ CUP

This quick-mix condiment is meant to accompany the buchimgae recipes in this book—the Kimchi Pancake (page 71), Onion Pancake (page 69), and Chrysanthemum Pancake (page 72). But it also works as a killer dipping sauce for Pork Dumplings (page 65) and as a dressing for Knife-Cut Noodles (page 120). The flavor profile of this sauce falls somewhere between the Chinese and Korean styles; think of a simple, satisfying, middle-of-the-road dish like Cantonese-style soy sauce noodles and you'll get the idea.

Whisk all ingredients in a bowl. Will keep in the refrigerator in a covered container for 1 week.

Soups

+

Stews

NOTHING CAPTURES THE TOTALITY OF KOREAN CUISINE QUITE LIKE ITS soups and stews. Unapologetic heat is the first trait many associate with Korean food, and that's certainly in play with jjigae, homestyle stews often spiked with red chili pepper. But there is so much more to explore, as the depth of this category illustrates so vividly. In Korean, the hardworking suffixes "guk" and "tang" describe a wide expanse of soups, ranging from spare, elegant broths that rival fine-dining consommé to hearty and harmonious combinations of meat, seafood, tofu, and vegetables.

Koreans assign great cultural weight to certain soups—for example, you're supposed to eat the rejuvenating miyeok-guk, Seaweed Soup (page 96), every birthday for good health. And while many Americans relegate their soupcraft to the fall and winter, it's a year-round affair around the Korean table, as soups encourage families to congregate around the communal pot. Keeping all this in mind, I've designed the recipes in this chapter—some traditional, others not—to feed anywhere from four to eight. If you're not cooking for a crowd, these are economical soups and stews that refrigerate and freeze well.

There's no right way to serve and eat the soups and stews that follow—and really, the same goes for any recipe in this book that feeds four or more. Do what makes sense to you. But here's how the typical Korean family might approach it. The communal pot's placed in the center of the table, and each eater is given their own bowl of steamed white rice, with individual portions of banchan and kimchi dished out, as well. Ladling a helping of the main dish right onto the rice and digging in is a common move. For a dish like my Whole Boiled Chicken Stew (page 87), however, I personally prefer it in a separate bowl. This keeps my plain rice plain as I incorporate it into my meal by the spoonful.

Anchovy Stock

4 sheets of dried kombu

6 cups cold water

18 dried anchovies, 4 inches long, heads and dried belly guts removed and discarded (about 150 grams)

MAKES 1 QUART

This briny, flavorful master broth has applications all over this book, from the Braised Seaweed Salad (page 36), Rolled Omelette (page 50), and Salmon and Kimchi (page 57) to this chapter's Crab Soup (page 100) and Seafood Stew (page 96). Unlike the White Pork Bone Broth that follows, this is more of a complementary ingredient than standalone. A little goes a long way.

Combine the kombu and 6 cups water in a large pot and leave it to soak, covered, for 30 minutes. Add the dried anchovies, then bring the pot to a boil. Cover, reduce the heat to low, and simmer for 15 minutes. Strain out the kombu and anchovies and allow the stock to cool. While the anchovies should be discarded, the kombu, after a quick rinse, can be used to make the Braised Seaweed Salad (page 36), or can be chopped and added to a soup, stew, or steamed rice.

To freeze, pour the completed stock in a freezer-safe vessel, such as a plastic quart container, and allow it to cool completely, uncovered, before transferring to the freezer, where it will keep for up to 3 months.

White Pork Bone Broth

2½ pounds pig's feet, split in half

18 cups water

NOTE: Don't be distressed if you discover that the light, milky end product doesn't taste like much upon completion—this means you did it correctly. Unlike more conventional stocks, the goal here is to draw the maximum amount of collagen, the structural protein that makes up most of the connective tissues in our bodies, from the pork; Koreans, along with many others, covet it for its purported health benefits. In traditional Korean restaurants, you can find this broth served with individual setups of salt, pepper, soy sauce, and scallions, allowing eaters to customize their seasoning.

MAKES ROUGHLY 3 QUARTS

This cloudy white bone broth is a staple of the Korean home cook. My mother-in-law makes a batch every other week, gently simmering a big ol' pot of pork trotters and water on her stovetop for a full day at minimum. It takes so long because slow and low is the only way to go when you're looking to completely break down the fat and skin of the trotters, known less fancifully as pig's feet, into a functional liquid form. The small, clean, separated bones that make up the trotters should be all that's left at the end of this process. For ease, seek out pre-split pig's feet, which you can find in ready-to-go packages in the meat section of most Asian groceries.

It's also a hugely valuable starting base for soups and stews (Kimchi-Pork Soup, page 86; "Instant" Ramyun for One, page 102), and really any recipe that calls for chicken stock (Bubbling Egg, page 59; Black Bean Noodles, page 122).

Place the pig's feet in a large pot and add just enough water to cover. No need to measure the water at this point. Place over high heat, uncovered, and bring to a full boil. Boil for 5 minutes. Discard the water, then rinse and scrub both the pig's feet and the pot itself—this will help remove any funky "barnyard" odors and flavors. Return the cleaned pig's feet to the pot and add the 18 cups water. Bring to a boil once again, then reduce the heat to low, add the lid, and simmer on the stovetop for 24 hours. Make sure the stovetop is clear of flammable material and everyone in your house, especially children, are aware that the burner will be on this long. Strain all bones out of the broth and discard them before serving or storing. Freeze it in 1-quart portions and thaw as needed; it will keep for up to 3 months.

Pork and Tomato Base

1 tablespoon vegetable oil

1 pound pork shoulder steak, cut into about 12 large chunks

1 tablespoon vegetable oil

½ large yellow onion, sliced

3 garlic cloves, sliced

1 cup chicken stock

One 28-ounce can crushed tomatoes

1 cup Master Kimchi Base (page 21)

MAKES 1 QUART

I've always loved the combination of pork, tomato, and kimchi, and I have been tinkering with it for years now in a professional setting. They just jive. I think it reminds me fondly of the classic spaghetti and meat sauce I grew up eating, with the kimchi thrown in to help me acknowledge, finally, that I am, in fact, Korean. A few years back we served a very popular stew at Serpico that juggled these powerful flavors with a few unexpected flourishes, like heirloom citrus, squid, and mussels. This recipe is a more accessible variation on the same idea. In addition to being cheap, a pork shoulder steak works really well for this, because you can get all the flavor without having to spend time trimming away the skin and bones that often accompany whole shoulders. This base can be enjoyed on its own, mixed into rice, but it also supercharges my Baked Eggs (page 61) and Seafood Stew (page 96).

In a large pot, heat the vegetable oil over medium heat. Brown the pork for 10 minutes, stirring occasionally. Add the onion and garlic, sweat for 10 minutes, then add the chicken stock, tomatoes, and Master Kimchi Base. Reduce heat to medium-low, cover, and simmer for 2 hours, until the liquid has darkened and reduced and the pork is very tender. Cool to room temperature before refrigerating or freezing.

Pork Belly and Cabbage Stew

8 ounces sliced pork belly, cut into bite-size pieces

½ medium yellow onion, sliced

2 garlic cloves, sliced

1 teaspoon kosher salt

4 cups chicken stock

One 14-ounce package firm tofu, cut into 1-inch cubes

3 cups Napa cabbage, diced (about 8 large leaves)

4 scallions, trimmed and cut into 2-inch pieces (white and light green parts)

Steamed rice and banchan of your choosing for serving

SERVES 4

This is a go-to of mine when I'm feeling under the weather, it's rainy/gray/miserable outside, or some combination of the two. It's mild and accessible in flavor, and takes well to the addition of vegetables: try broccoli, mushrooms, or lettuce. Working with pork belly might be intimidating if you're unfamiliar with the cut, but remember that it's just bacon in its pre-smoked infancy. In fact, you could substitute a like amount of uncured bacon, which will give it more of a Chinese delivery vibe (just pay attention to how much additional salt you incorporate, in this case). Korean groceries often sell pork belly pre-sliced into the size you want here, but good butcher shops will be happy to slice it for you to order.

In a large pot, add the pork belly, onion, garlic, and salt and cook for 10 minutes over medium heat, stirring occasionally, until both the pork and onion start gaining some color. Spoon out any excess fat, then add all the remaining ingredients to the pot. Turn the heat to high and bring the stew to a boil, then reduce heat to medium, cover, and cook for 20 minutes, until the cabbage and onions are tender and translucent. Serve with steamed rice and Potato Sticks (page 34), Marinated Mushrooms (page 38), or any other banchan you like.

Easy Pork Shoulder Stew

1½ pounds boneless pork shoulder, cut into 1-inch chunks

4 cups chicken stock

4 cups water

One 14-ounce package firm tofu, cut into 1-inch cubes

1 large or 3 to 4 medium carrots, peeled and cut into 1-inch pieces (about ½ pound)

½ head green cabbage, chopped

1 bunch scallions, trimmed and cut into 1-inch pieces (white and light green parts)

5 garlic cloves, sliced

1 tablespoon peeled, minced ginger

¼ cup fermented bean paste

1 tablespoon Korean chili powder

1 tablespoon kosher salt

SERVES 4

This stew is a perfect "just make it happen" meal when you are in a pinch but still want to come up with something hearty and satisfying. It comes together well without much stress thanks to a few quick tricks I've massaged into the recipe itself. By including vegetables like carrots and cabbage, you're essentially making a rich stock and cooking a stew simultaneously, maximizing the efficiency of your time in the kitchen. Pork shoulder is a means to this end, too. It's one of the absolute best cuts of meat money can buy, though it always takes a little time to achieve the ideal tender-simmered bite and flavorful, rendered fat. Tossing everything into one big pot and just letting it go gets the job done with little fuss. Ask for a boneless shoulder, skin removed, so it's easier to break down at home.

Add the pork shoulder to a large pot and cover with cold water. Bring to a boil, boil 1 minute, then remove the pork, discard the water, and rinse the pot thoroughly—this will help remove any funky "barnyard" odors and flavors. Return the pork to the pot, cover with the chicken stock and 4 cups water, then bring back to a boil. Add the remaining ingredients, stirring gently to combine. Reduce heat to a slow simmer, cover the pot, and cook for 1 hour and 45 minutes, or until the pork is tender but not falling apart. Taste the stew for salt before serving, adjusting if necessary.

Spicy Pork Rib Stew

1 rack baby back ribs (2 to 3 pounds), cut into 1-bone pieces

1 medium yellow onion, sliced

5 garlic cloves, sliced

½ cup Korean chili paste

¼ cup Korean chili flake

¼ cup fermented bean paste

8 cups cold water

1 tablespoon kosher salt

2 tablespoons soy sauce

1 tablespoon sesame oil

1 tablespoon honey

3 Yukon gold potatoes, unpeeled and cut into large chunks

1 bunch scallions, trimmed and cut into 2-inch pieces (white and light green parts)

½ head green cabbage, cut into large chunks

¼ cup ground perilla seed (optional)

Steamed rice and banchan of your choosing for serving

SERVES 6 TO 8

This is my interpretation of gamjatang, a beloved stew that goes back centuries to hog farmers in the southernmost province of Korea. It's a working person's meal that relies on humbler cuts of pork, frequently from the spine and neck, along with hearty cabbage and potatoes in a pleasantly salty, plenty-spicy broth. I've swapped in baby back pork ribs for neck bones—easier to find in grocery stores and very easy to butcher, without sacrificing any fat or flavor. Yes, this is a pork lover's dish, but the most perplexing flavor of a traditional gamjatang comes from an ingredient you might not know: ground perilla seed. Sometimes confused with sesame, perilla actually belongs to the mint family, which explains its medicinal pop. With leaves and seeds used widely in Korean cuisine, it's also got an earthy character that will appeal to fans of fennel and black peppercorn. Adding it is optional in this recipe. I personally love it.

Combine all ingredients except potatoes, scallion, cabbage, and perilla seed (if using) in a large, heavy pot and bring to a boil. Once boiling, reduce heat to low and cover. Slowly simmer for 1½ hours, until the ribs are just about ready to come off the bone. Skim fat off the top of the stew, then add potatoes, scallion, and cabbage. Return heat to high and boil for 30 more minutes, uncovered, until potatoes are cooked. Top with ground perilla seed, if using, just before serving. Serve hot with steamed rice and banchan of your choosing. I recommend Quick-Cured Cucumbers (page 32) and Battered Zucchini (page 46).

Kimchi-Pork Soup

½ pound pork belly, sliced into small, thin squares

4 garlic cloves, sliced

1 medium yellow onion, sliced

1 cup Countertop Kimchi (page 13)

6 cups White Pork Bone Broth (page 79), chicken stock, or water

½ teaspoon kosher salt

½ teaspoon soy sauce

Steamed rice and banchan of your choosing for serving

SERVES 4

This is a satisfying soup I conjure up for my family when we have "nothing in the house"—a classic weeknight dilemma for us, and I'm sure many others. We always keep frozen pre-sliced pork belly in our freezer and homemade kimchi in our fridge, so I tend to just snag some of the meat and cook it directly from its frozen state. Couldn't be easier, and unlike some other soups and stews in this chapter, it comes together in minutes. The kimchi lends the tang and crunch we all crave, and I'll even toss frozen mixed veggies into this, too—I know that's the opposite of "cheffy," but sometimes you just gotta work with what you got.

Combine all ingredients in a medium saucepan, bring to a boil, and cook for 10 minutes. Serve with steamed rice and banchan of your choosing. I recommend Braised Seaweed Salad (page 36) and Perfect Soft-Boiled Egg (page 48).

Whole Boiled Chicken Stew

One 4-pound whole chicken

1 medium yellow onion, sliced

3 garlic cloves, sliced

1 large or 3 to 4 medium carrots, peeled and cut into large rounds (about ½ pound)

6 dried shiitake mushrooms

2 tablespoons fermented bean paste

2 tablespoons soy sauce

2 tablespoons kosher salt

¼ teaspoon ground black pepper

1 tablespoon Korean chili flake

9 cups water

2 tablespoons mirin

Steamed rice, kimchi, and banchan of your choosing for serving

SERVES 6 TO 8

I see this as my chicken soup for the overworked chef/dad's soul (minus the noodles). There can be a lot of guesswork and moving parts to roasting a whole chicken, though it's usually worth the slight trouble. This is the move when you just don't have it in you to fuss. It's a one-pot, one-shot deal, it feeds a crowd, and it produces leftover chicken aplenty that can be remixed in all sorts of ways (sandwiches, salads, stir-fries, etc.). Don't worry if the breast portion of the chicken isn't completely covered by liquid, it'll cook. Note that I have gone light on the salt as a starting point here. You might want more based on your personal preferences, but it's always a better bet to start small and season to taste, as opposed to scrambling to fix a way-oversalted broth after a long cooking time.

Combine the chicken, breast-side up, and all other ingredients in a large pot and bring to a boil. Reduce heat to medium-low, cover, and simmer for 1 hour. After 1 hour, turn off the heat and allow the pot to rest, lid on, for an additional hour. Remove the chicken from the pot and, wearing gloves, pick off all the meat. Discard the carcass, skin, and bones, or reserve them for a batch of chicken stock. Using scissors, cut the now-cooked shiitake mushrooms into bite-size pieces over the pot, then add the picked chicken meat back into the stew. Serve with steamed rice, kimchi, and banchan of your choosing. I recommend Marinated Tofu (page 43) and Sweet and Salty Soybeans (page 53).

Beef and Radish Stew

1½ pounds beef short ribs, with the bones cut 3 to 4 inches long

4 cups beef stock

8 cups water

1 medium daikon radish, peeled and sliced into ¼-inch rounds (about 1 pound)

1 teaspoon peeled, chopped ginger

3 garlic cloves, sliced

1 tablespoon fish sauce

1 tablespoon soy sauce

1 tablespoon kosher salt

SERVES 4

Many wrongly assume that Korean food is exclusively funky and spicy, which is why I love this stew, an old-school mainstay (soegogi-muguk) that's one of Julie's favorites. She makes it frequently throughout the winter, never relying on a recipe, so I knew I had my work cut out for me developing this rendition. This is a pure expression of Korean-style cooking—so clean, and at once hearty and light. The beef only gets better the longer you cook it, and though fish sauce might not strike you as a logical partner for short rib bones, these deep, distinct flavors collaborate quite well. The sneaky all-star here, though, is the spoon-tender braised daikon. In addition to adding complexity to the broth itself, slow-cooking coaxes out a quiet sweetness in the radishes, while still maintaining a touch of their appealing natural bitterness. Think of it as the Korean answer to adding chunked potatoes to a homey beef stew—daikon won't thicken the broth the same way, given the comparative lack of starch, but it still warms and satisfies.

Add short ribs to a large pot and cover them in cold water. Bring to a boil, boil for 1 minute, then turn off heat, remove the meat with tongs or a slotted spoon, discard water, and rinse out the pot—this will help remove any funky "barnyard" odors and flavors. Return the short ribs to the pot, covering them in beef stock and adding the 8 cups water. Return to a boil and add all remaining ingredients. Reduce heat to a slow simmer, cover, and simmer for 1 hour and 45 minutes; the broth will be lightly fragrant and the beef will be close to separating from the bone. Serve with banchan and rice. Store in a container in the refrigerator or just keep it in the pot in the fridge once it has cooled.

Spicy Skirt Steak Stew

1 pound skirt steak, trimmed, and cut into 1-inch pieces

8 button mushrooms, sliced

6 dried shiitake mushrooms

½ medium yellow onion, sliced

3 garlic cloves, sliced

8 scallions, trimmed and cut into 2-inch pieces (white and light green parts)

3 cups water

1 teaspoon kosher salt

1 teaspoon Korean chili flake

3 tablespoons Korean chili paste

1 tablespoon mirin

1 tablespoon maple syrup

1 teaspoon sesame oil

SERVES 4

Occupying the opposite end of the capsaicin spectrum from my Beef and Radish Stew is this easy-to-execute complement, which brings the heat via generous chili flake and chili paste, counterbalanced by maple syrup and umami-bomb mushrooms. It's a wonderful setup for the naturally tougher skirt steak, which is very braise-friendly. This is not a cut of beef you see used very often in Korean cuisine, but I wanted to develop ways to use it, since groceries and butcher shops always have it on hand. As is the case with many of the soups and stews found throughout this chapter, meat does not serve as the marquee star—it's an accompaniment, a consummate team player. The selling point is the stew as a whole, not just the steak.

In a pot, combine the skirt steak, mushrooms, onion, scallions, garlic, water, and salt and bring to a boil. Reduce the heat to low, cover, and simmer for 3 hours. Add the chili flake, chili paste, mirin, maple syrup, and sesame oil. Continue to simmer on low for an additional 30 minutes; the beef will be delicate and tender, and the reduced broth should have a bold and concentrated flavor. Serve with steamed rice, kimchi, and banchan of your choosing. I recommend Pickled Iceberg Lettuce (page 39) and Burdock Root (page 47).

Oxtail Vegetable Stew

2 pounds oxtail, cut into 2-inch pieces

10 cups water

8 dried shiitake mushrooms, chopped

1 large Idaho potato, peeled, halved, then cut into 1-inch half-moons

1 medium daikon radish, peeled, halved lengthwise, and cut into 1-inch half-moons (about 1 pound)

3 cups Napa cabbage (about 5 to 6 leaves), halved lengthwise, then rough-chopped

6 scallions, trimmed and cut into 1-inch pieces (white and light green parts)

2 tablespoons soy sauce

2 tablespoons kosher salt

Black Pepper Oil (page 175)

SERVES 4 TO 6

I find myself craving this stew the second I feel a chill in the air. It's packed with substantial veggies—mushrooms, potatoes, daikon, Napa cabbage—that complement the unctuous, soul-affirming nature of oxtail. For the longest time, the fatty, luscious cut was the domain of Asian, African, Caribbean, and Latin home cooking traditions, but ever since high-end restaurant chefs starting messing around with it, it's gotten pricier, and a little more scarce (a cow's only got one tail, after all). A good place to find some is in the frozen section of Asian grocery stores, already butchered into rounds and ready to rock. Look for packages with a mix of large and small pieces. While big oxtail segments provide ample meat and marrow, the more delicate small rounds, taken from where the tail starts to taper, break down more during cooking, deepening the beefy flavor. To up the rib-sticking value of this stew even more, incorporate my "Cheesy" Rice Cakes (page 117), top with a Perfect Hard-Boiled Egg (page 48), or serve with a side of Knife-Cut Noodles (page 120).

Add the oxtail to a large pot, cover with water, and boil for 5 minutes. Using tongs or a slotted spoon, remove the oxtail and rinse under cold water, discarding any bone shards, then scrub out the pot—this will help remove any funky "barnyard" odors and flavors. Return the oxtail to the pot and add the 10 cups water and dried shiitakes. Bring to a boil. Reduce heat to low, cover, and simmer for 2½ hours, skimming any fat off the top if necessary. Add the potato, daikon, cabbage, scallion, soy sauce, and salt and simmer for an additional 30 minutes, until the potato and daikon are fork-tender. Garnish with Black Pepper Oil.

Easy Stovetop Rice (page 129)

Mu Radish Kimchi (page 27)

Oxtail Vegetable Soup (page 90)

Oxtail Soup

2 pounds oxtail, cut into 2-inch pieces

12 cups water or stock

2 scallions, trimmed and sliced (white and light green parts)

Black pepper to taste

Kosher salt to taste

SERVES 4

Many of the dishes in this book are nontraditional, but this soup is quite close to a classic preparation called kkori-gomtang. For lack of a better term, this is technically a "bland" soup, and that is deliberate. The long cooking time, involving nothing more than the oxtails and a base of unseasoned water for its majority, succeeds in drawing the maximum richness from the bones and cartilage, creating a delicate, meditative broth. (See page 90 for oxtail shopping tips.) Serve individual portions with condiment setups of salt, black pepper (or Black Pepper Oil, page 175), and sliced scallion, so each person can customize their bowl to their individual tastes. Everyone will dress this soup up a little differently, and that's the beauty of this format. I like to go light on the salt and pepper, preferring to pair a subtler broth with pops of flavor from my kimchi and banchan. You, however, might discover that a heavier hand is what you like best. Incorporate salt and pepper into your broth a little at a time to find your happy place, and remember that you can always add more if need be.

Add the oxtail to a large pot, cover with water, and boil for 5 minutes. Remove the oxtail and rinse under cold water, discarding any bone shards, and scrub out the pot—this will help remove any funky "barnyard" odors and flavors. Return the oxtail to the pot and add the 12 cups water. Bring back to a boil, then reduce heat to low, cover, and simmer for 4 hours, skimming any fat off the top if necessary. Increase the heat to medium-low, cover, and cook for an additional 30 minutes. Garnish the soup with scallions and season with black pepper and kosher salt to taste.

Easy Stovetop Rice (page 129)

Bok Choy Kimchi (page 18)

Black Pepper Oil (page 175)

Oxtail Soup (page 92)

Korean Army Stew

For the sauce

2 tablespoons Korean chili flake

2 tablespoons mirin

1 tablespoon soy sauce

3 garlic cloves, sliced

2 teaspoon sugar

2 teaspoons Korean chili paste

½ teaspoon ground black pepper or Black Pepper Oil (page 175)

For the stew

6 ounces Spam, cut into bite-size slices

2 hot dogs, each sliced on the bias into 5 pieces

One 14-ounce package firm tofu, cut into bite-size slices

3 ounces enoki mushrooms

1 cup fresh shiitake mushrooms, stems removed and discarded, caps sliced thin

4 scallions, trimmed and cut into 2-inch pieces (white and light green parts)

½ cup Countertop Kimchi (page 13)

4 cups chicken stock

1 package instant Korean noodles (like Shin Ramyun)

4 slices American cheese (like Kraft Singles)

SERVES 4

Budae jjigae, or "army base stew," came about in the years following the Korean War, which devastated the entire peninsula for decades. The story goes that impoverished Koreans hired to cook for US military installations in the city of Uijeongbu would smuggle out American products left uneaten by GIs—hot dogs, baked beans, Vienna sausages, yellow cheese, Spam—eventually combining them with native ingredients like kimchi and gochujang to create this dish. Interestingly, this byproduct of a dark period in Korea's history became extremely popular with Koreans, especially as drunk food with friends. (Uijeongbu has an actual "Budae Jjigae Street," populated by dozens of restaurants specializing in it.) I know this stew, packed with processed meats, doesn't exactly jibe with the healthier approach I take elsewhere in this book, but I like that it represents resilience. Plus, it's neither all the way Korean, nor all the way American—something I can certainly relate to.

Whisk together the ingredients for the sauce in a small mixing bowl and set aside.

Fan out all the ingredients for the stew, except the chicken stock, noodles, and American cheese, around the circumference of a large pot, leaving a small open area in the middle. Add the whisked sauce into this space, pour the chicken stock over it, and bring the stew to a boil for 5 minutes, until the mushrooms are cooked through. Add the noodles and cook for 3 more minutes. Top with the cheese and serve immediately, bringing the entire pot over to the table and letting your friends serve themselves.

Seafood Stew

1¾ cups Pork and Tomato Base (page 80)

1¾ cups Anchovy Stock (page 78)

2 cups Napa cabbage (about 4 leaves), halved lengthwise, then rough-chopped

½ block firm tofu, cut into bite-size pieces

1 tablespoon Korean chili flake

2 cups frozen seafood blend (scallop, shrimp, squid)

Steamed rice for serving

SERVES 4 TO 6

Though fresh seafood will work wonderfully for this Korean-style "surf and turf" situation, I've found that a frozen seafood mix (shrimp, mussels, scallops, squid)—the type carried at Asian and general grocery stores alike—is a huge time-saver. Look for a product that is "individually quick frozen" (IQF)—that way, it won't get freezer-burned or turn into an unwieldy block of ice that takes forever to thaw. If you're going with fresh, I suggest sticking to a single type of fish or seafood—say shrimp, or fillets of haddock or cod, in lieu of a variety—to ensure even cooking. Note that fresh stuff will finish cooking even faster than the 5 minutes I've allotted for frozen.

Add all ingredients except the seafood to a large pot and boil for 5 minutes, until the cabbage is cooked. Add the frozen seafood mix to the pot and boil for another 5 minutes. Serve immediately with steamed rice.

Seafood Stew (page 96)

White Kimchi (page 26)

Clam Soup

2 pounds manila clams
(about 20 clams)

4 cups water

2 scallions, trimmed and
cut into 1-inch pieces
(white and light green parts)

3 garlic cloves, sliced

1 small jalapeño pepper,
seeded and sliced

1 tablespoon fermented bean
paste

½ block firm tofu, cut into
¼-inch cubes

Steamed rice and banchan of
your choosing for serving

SERVES 4

Clams are one of my absolute favorite things—not just the mollusks themselves, but the broth you get as a reward for cooking them correctly. To me, this stuff is liquid gold, so perfectly salty and a little sweet. There are so many variations on jogaetang out there, but the best I've tried have the cleanest, clearest, sparest broths. The less you do to it, the better. With that in mind, I've kept this recipe pretty basic, both to maximize that flavor I crave and to account for the fact that different clams will give you different levels of salinity, depending on where they're harvested. Feel free to add additional salt or soy sauce at the end, if you feel like your soup needs more seasoning.

Scrub the clams well under running water to remove as much excess sand and grit from their shells as possible. Make sure all the clams are closed tightly, discarding any that are cracked, broken, or open. Bring the 4 cups water to a boil in a large pot and add the clams. Once they open up (5 to 6 minutes, give or take), transfer them to a large serving bowl with a slotted spoon. Line a fine-mesh strainer with a double layer of paper towels and place it over another bowl. Strain the liquid from the pot into the bowl to catch any additional grit and sand expelled by the clams. Rinse out the large pot, then return the strained, clean broth to the pot. Bring this broth to a boil, then add all remaining ingredients. Boil for 5 minutes, then pour the contents of the pot into the bowl of clams. Serve immediately with steamed rice and banchan of your choosing. I recommend Steamed Eggplant (page 44) and Roasted Beech Mushrooms (page 45).

Easy Stovetop Rice (page 129)

Countertop Kimchi (page 13)

Clam Soup (page 98)

Crab Soup

5 cups water or chicken stock

1 cup Anchovy Stock
(page 78)

1 medium daikon radish,
peeled and sliced into 1-inch
half-moons (about 1 pound)

½ large yellow onion, sliced

4 garlic cloves, sliced

2 tablespoons fermented bean
paste

1 tablespoon Korean chili paste

3 Korean chili peppers,
stemmed, seeded, sliced

1 teaspoon kosher salt

1½ pounds whole blue crabs,
thawed (if frozen)

1 small zucchini, cut into
½-inch half-moons

3 scallions, trimmed and
sliced into thin, wispy ribbons
(white and light green parts)

1 cup fresh chrysanthemum,
leaves and stems, chopped

Steamed rice for serving

SERVES 6

Here's my interpretation of my mother-in-law's special recipe, which is another one of Julie's favorite dishes. When she was a kid, her father would take her to his secret spot on Long Island and trap blue crabs specifically to make this bright but balanced soup, which is plenty spicy, but not so much that you miss out on that incredibly distinct, briny-sweet crab essence. Being from Maryland, I'm very familiar with how expensive and temperamental live blues can be, so I'm more than fine with frozen crabs, since they are much easier to secure and work with. Grassy and refreshing in flavor, chrysanthemum, called ssukgat or crown daisy, is common in Korea both as banchan and as a garnish, often for seafood. Use any leftover leaves and stems to make a Chrysanthemum Pancake (page 72).

In a large lidded pot, bring the water/chicken stock, Anchovy Stock, daikon, onion, garlic, fermented bean paste, chili paste, chili peppers, and salt to a boil. Reduce the heat to low, cover, and simmer for 10 minutes, until the daikon is slightly tender. Add the crabs, zucchini, scallion, and chrysanthemum, increase heat to high, and boil for 10 minutes. Serve immediately, preferably ladling into individual bowls while it's still boiling, with steamed white rice.

Mushroom and Cabbage Soup

8 cups water or vegetable stock

3 cups Napa cabbage (about 5 to 6 leaves), halved lengthwise, then rough-chopped

10 dried shiitake mushrooms, sliced

8 ounces button mushrooms, sliced

One 14-ounce package firm tofu, cut into 1-inch cubes

2 garlic cloves, sliced

½ large yellow onion, sliced

1 tablespoon kosher salt

SERVES 4

This is a straightforward (and customizable) vegan soup that draws big flavor from Napa cabbage and two types of mushrooms—readily available buttons, an easy way to bump up each bite; and dried shiitakes, one of my favorite and most reliable sources of concentrated umami. The first time you try this recipe, I suggest adding everything to the pot simultaneously, then bringing it to a boil, as instructed. But as you get more comfortable, one time-saving tip is to heat your water or stock while you prep all the other ingredients. The liquid will hit its boiling point faster on its own, at which point you can toss everything you just chopped up in; it'll speed the whole process up considerably.

Add all ingredients to a large pot and bring to a boil. Reduce the heat to medium and simmer for 45 minutes, until the broth has reduced and is round and balanced in flavor. Serve immediately.

"Instant" Ramyun for One

2 cups water or chicken stock

1 dried shiitake mushroom, chopped

1 garlic clove, sliced

1 scallion, trimmed and sliced into thin, wispy ribbons (white and light green parts)

½ teaspoon kosher salt

¼ cup Countertop Kimchi (page 13) plus 1 tablespoon kimchi liquid

1 teaspoon soy sauce

¼ teaspoon Korean chili flake

2 teaspoons mirin

1 package instant Korean noodles

Perfect Soft-Boiled Egg (page 48) for garnish (optional)

Braised Pork Belly (page 155) for garnish (optional)

SERVES 1

Instant ramyun is hugely popular in South Korea—and just like Cup Noodles, the packets are absolutely packed with sodium and preservatives. This is a half-recipe "hack" of sorts that'll turn out a far healthier and tastier alternative. If you were to do a soup like this from scratch, the noodles would definitely be the trickiest part. Tagging in dried noodles while crafting your own broth is the logical move. In lieu of water or stock, experiment with Anchovy Stock (page 78) or White Pork Bone Broth (page 79), or even combinations thereof.

Add all ingredients except the instant noodles and optional garnishes to a medium pot and bring to a boil. Add the brick of dried instant noodles to the pot and cook them according to the package instructions—typically, that's 4 minutes for a stiffer texture, and 5 minutes for softer noodles. Garnish with Perfect Soft-Boiled Egg and Braised Pork Belly if you'd like, or just enjoy on its own.

Acorn Squash Soup

1 acorn squash (approximately 1½ pounds)

1 tablespoon vegetable oil

1 tablespoon fermented bean paste

1 tablespoon maple syrup

1 cup chicken stock or vegetable stock

2 cups water

1 teaspoon kosher salt

½ recipe Crispy Rice Cakes (page 113)

1 tablespoon pumpkin seeds for garnish

SERVES 4

This is a relatively classic approach to making hobak-juk, a Korean porridge most commonly featuring pumpkin or kabocha squash. I like to use acorn squash because it's a little easier to work with—baking it beforehand is absolutely key—and it seems to be more readily available in stores. Dropping the rice cakes into the soup creates a thick, noodly, gnocchi-type sensation that will appeal to anyone who loves the Italian grandma school of cooking (aka me).

Preheat the oven to 350°F. Slice acorn squash in half lengthwise, scooping out and discarding all seeds and soft pulp. Rub the exposed insides of the squash with the vegetable oil in a thin layer, place it flesh side up on a small baking sheet, and bake for 1 hour. Allow to cool, then scoop its flesh out into a blender, along with all other ingredients except for the Crispy Rice Cakes and pumpkin seeds, and puree until smooth. Pour puree into a medium pot. Heat the pot over medium heat, then add the Crispy Rice Cakes and simmer for 10 to 15 minutes, until the rice cakes are cooked through. This will help thicken the soup slightly. Garnish with pumpkin seeds and serve immediately.

Easy Stovetop Rice (page 129)

Countertop Kimchi (page 13)

Marinated Bean Sprouts (page 37)

Seaweed Soup (page 96)

Seaweed Soup

½ cup dried seaweed (look for Ottogi brand "Cut Seaweed")

6 cups water or chicken stock

2 boneless, skinless chicken breasts

6 garlic cloves, sliced

1 teaspoon peeled, minced ginger

1 tablespoon fish sauce

1 teaspoon kosher salt

Steamed rice for serving

SERVES 4

This dish, called miyeok-guk, is very important in Korean culture. You eat it on your birthday to commemorate another year of life. It's traditionally pretty mild, and I didn't think much of it the first time I tried it, but it started growing on me because it's one of my wife and daughter's favorites. Julie will put this on the stovetop, go to pick up Charlie from school nearby, and by the time they're back it's done. It's one of the few dishes Charlie asks for specifically, proving she is more Korean than I am. This is a base recipe; in the past, we've added thin strips of beef, enoki and hon shimeji mushrooms, and more.

In a large pot, soak the dried seaweed in the water or chicken stock for 10 minutes without heat. Add all the remaining ingredients, turn heat to high, and boil for 15 minutes. Remove the cooked chicken breasts from the soup, cut them into bite-size pieces with a knife or scissors and return them to the pot. Season the soup with fish sauce and kosher salt before serving alongside steamed rice.

Rice + Noodles

WHEN IT COMES TO RICE AND NOODLES, I CAN PROUDLY SAY THAT I, Peter Serpico, am a Korean grandma. I'm not proclaiming that I'm better at cooking than the local Halmonis in your life—I wouldn't dare. What I'm trying to say is that, when it comes to carbohydrates of the Korean persuasion, I prefer simple, honest, straightforward preparations that let me work with my hands and aren't too concerned with phony Instagram flashiness. Remember: even a dish that's unassuming in makeup and execution can taste transcendent with the right amount of patience and care.

I cover all the classics in this chapter, including two techniques for making from scratch duk boki, Korean rice cakes (pages 113 and 117), and my takes on the always-popular japchae (page 126), bibimguksu (page 124), jajangmyeon (page 122), and bibimbap (page 137). And, in addition to a few of my own nontraditional recipes, I'll walk you through the absolute basics of making rice (page 129), something people always ask me about. I hope you draw as much comfort and satisfaction from eating these dishes as I did from developing them.

Crispy Rice Cakes (page 113)

"Cheesy" Rice Cakes (page 117)

Knife-Cut Noodles (page 120)

Acorn Squash Soup (page 104)

Rice Sticks with Beef (page 118)

Crispy Rice Cakes with Sauce

For the Sauce

1 tablespoon sesame oil

½ medium yellow onion, sliced

1 garlic clove, minced

½ cup Anchovy Stock (page 78), chicken stock, vegetable stock, or water

2 teaspoons Korean chili paste

2 teaspoons soy sauce

½ teaspoon Korean chili flake

2 teaspoons sugar

1 tablespoon white sesame seeds

For the Rice Cakes

½ cup rice flour

½ cup glutinous rice flour

¼ cup water, with more reserved

¼ teaspoon kosher salt

1 tablespoon vegetable oil for frying

2 scallions, trimmed and sliced into thin, wispy ribbons (white and light green parts) for garnish

SERVES 2 (MAKES 8 RICE CAKES)

This is my at-home version of duk boki, the versatile Korean rice cakes coveted for their crispy texture. Don't think of those boring low-calorie Quaker Oats snacks when you hear "rice cake" in this instance. Picture instead dumplings of varying size and shape that are adept at absorbing and retaining flavor. They can be prepared in many different ways; for this first of two techniques, we're hand-rolling and panfrying them in sticks. For the second technique, see page 117. The combination of regular rice flour and glutinous rice flour is essential for this recipe. Don't substitute anything or your cakes will turn brittle. The unique starch structure of glutinous rice is what gives Korean rice cakes their appealing bounce. Along with the spicy sauce detailed below (make it first), this is a meal unto itself, but the duk boki on their own are also a component of my Acorn Squash Soup (page 104) and Rice Sticks with Beef (page 118).

First make the sauce. In a small saucepan, heat the sesame oil over medium heat, then sauté the onion until slightly wilted, about 3 minutes. Add garlic and sauté for 1 minute. Add stock or water, then all remaining ingredients, increase heat to high and boil, stirring occasionally, until the sauce has thickened and reduced by half, about 15 minutes.

Make the rice cakes next. Combine the flours, ¼ cup water, and salt in a microwave-safe bowl. There's no need to mix it. Microwave on high for 1 minute, then turn the contents of the bowl out onto an unfloured work surface. Knead this mass to form a smooth dough, trickling in small amounts of the reserved water if necessary to help incorporate all the flour evenly. Cut the dough in half, halve each piece, then halve these pieces once more, creating eight even portions. Gently roll each piece

recipe continues $\longrightarrow$

After microwaving, turn the flour-water-salt mixture out onto a clean work surface.

Knead into a dough. If the mixture is too dry, trickle in a little water, but do so sparingly.

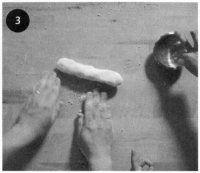

The dough is ready once all flour has been incorporated and it has a smooth, uniform texture.

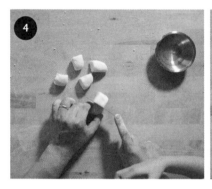

Cut the dough in half, halve each piece, then halve each piece again . . .

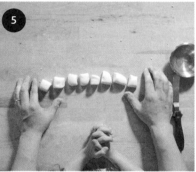

. . . creating eight even portions.

Gently roll each piece of dough into a stick the length of your middle finger.

Drop the newly formed rice cakes into boiling water for 2 to 3 minutes. While waiting, add the vegetable oil in a large nonstick pan over medium heat.

Transfer boiled rice cakes into the hot pan, browning each side for 1 minute.

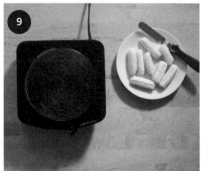

Finished rice sticks.

into a stick the length of your middle finger. (At this point, you can refrigerate or freeze the rice cakes for later preparation.) In a medium saucepan, bring some water to a boil and drop in the rice cakes for 2 to 3 minutes. While they're boiling, heat the vegetable oil in a large nonstick pan over medium heat. Using tongs or a slotted spoon, gently transfer the rice cakes directly from the boiling water into the hot pan, being careful not to splatter. They'll stick together if they touch, so give them ample room. Brown the rice cakes on each side for 1 minute, then transfer them to a paper towel-lined plate to drain. They will be gooey in texture right out of the pan, so let them cool slightly before moving them to a serving plate, pouring the sauce over top and garnishing with sliced scallions.

"Cheesy" Rice Cakes

1½ cups glutinous rice flour

¾ cup boiling water

1 tablespoon kosher salt

2 tablespoons vegetable oil, for frying

SERVES 2 (MAKES ABOUT 16 RICE CAKES)

The dough-making process for this particular duk boki, combined with a tweaked flour-to-water ratio, creates a gummy, chewy texture I'd compare to mozzarella—that's why I like to distinguish these as "cheesy," even though there's no actual dairy involved here. The simple two-spoon technique detailed in the instructions keeps the size and shape of your rice cakes relatively uniform, though a little variety never hurt anybody, so don't stress over variation too much. More importantly, it also prevents a giant mess. I have created one or two of those over the years, so I'm always glad to avoid them. For planning purposes, note that the dough needs to rest for 30 minutes before forming and cooking the rice cakes.

Combine the glutinous rice flour, boiling water, and salt in a large bowl and mix together well with a large wooden spoon—it will be sticky and hot, so be careful. Let the bowl stand, uncovered, at room temperature for 30 minutes to allow the flour to hydrate. After 30 minutes, add the vegetable oil to a pan or skillet over medium-high heat. Use two large metal tablespoons to form your cheesy rice cakes straight from the bowl—the first spoon to scoop and shape, the second to gently ease the rice cake off the first spoon into the hot oil. Fry rice cakes for 3 minutes on each side, then remove and drain them on a paper towel. Eat warm by themselves, or with the chili sauce that accompanies the Crispy Rice Cakes (page 113).

Rice Sticks with Beef

8 Crispy Rice Cakes (page 113)

2 tablespoons vegetable oil, plus more to brown the rice cakes

8 ounces sirloin, cleaned of fat and gristle, thinly sliced

½ teaspoon freshly ground pepper

3 tablespoons soy sauce

2 garlic cloves, sliced

1 tablespoon sesame oil

1 tablespoon raw sugar or brown sugar

2 tablespoons chicken stock or water

2 scallions, trimmed and thinly sliced (white and light green parts)

SERVES 4

Here's a rice cake setup for those of you looking for something a little less spicy. In lieu of a hot chili sauce, you'll be whipping up a salty, savory stir-fry featuring slivers of steak quick-marinated in soy sauce, garlic, sugar, and scallion. I've chosen to use sirloin here for a few reasons. It's a super-flavorful cut of beef, of course, but it's also extremely easy to work with at home. Here's a trick I've borrowed from Philadelphia's excellent cheesesteak shops to streamline your prep: Pop your cleaned-up meat in the freezer for about 15 minutes prior to slicing it up. It will firm up the beef just enough to help you produce thin, uniform cuts that will cook quickly and evenly.

In a small bowl, combine all ingredients except for the sesame oil, chicken stock, and scallions and allow the sirloin to marinate. Then boil and panfry the Crispy Rice Cakes per the recipe (page 113): In a medium saucepan, bring some water to a boil and drop in the rice cakes for 2 to 3 minutes. While they're boiling, heat some vegetable oil in a large nonstick pan over medium heat. Using tongs or a slotted spoon, gently move the rice cakes directly from the boiling water into the hot pan, being careful not to splatter. They'll stick together if they touch, so give them ample room. Brown the rice cakes on each side for 1 minute, then transfer them to a serving plate.

In a skillet, heat the sesame oil over medium-high heat, then add the marinated sirloin and chicken stock or water. Sauté until the beef has cooked through and is lightly caramelized, and the liquid is nearly evaporated, about 5 minutes. Pour the contents of the skillet over the cooked rice sticks and garnish with sliced scallions.

Hand-Pulled Noodles in Broth

For the Noodles

¾ cup water

1 teaspoon soy sauce

1 tablespoon sesame oil

2 cups all-purpose flour

For the Broth

6 cups chicken stock or Anchovy Stock (page 78)

3 scallions, trimmed and cut into 1-inch pieces (white and light green parts)

1 cup frozen vegetable mix (carrots, corn, green beans, peas)

SERVES 4

Hand-pulled noodles are the key ingredient in sujebi, a comforting soup often associated with the working class. It's prepared by flinging pieces of raw dough into a bubbling broth, placing them somewhere between German spätzle and Chinese dao xiao mian (Shanxi shaved noodles) on the blue-collar carb scale. Soy and sesame distinguishes these noodles from their knife-cut cousins (page 120), while the shaping and cooking process creates a distinct chew. (Heads up: The dough requires at least 1 hour to rest, so plan accordingly.) Though not traditional, I'd recommend cooking your noodles in boiling water separate from your broth, as the starch might thicken it too much. Hand-pulled noodles are also great with Anything Sauce (page 178) and Ground Beef Bulgogi (page 159), or just simply tossed with more soy sauce and sesame oil.

In a stand mixer equipped with a dough hook attachment, combine the water, soy sauce, sesame oil, and all-purpose flour and mix, starting on slow and gradually increasing speed until fully incorporated. (If you don't have a stand mixer, combine the ingredients in a large bowl and mix them together with a large spoon.) Cover the bowl with plastic wrap, then allow the dough to rest and hydrate for a minimum of 1 hour. Rip off small pieces from the dough, about the size of one-quarter of a dollar bill, and stretch them as thinly as you can without ripping them. Collect the stretched noodles on a plate.

Bring a pot of water to a boil; combine all the ingredients for the broth in a second pot and bring that to a boil as well. Add the stretched noodles to the boiling water, cook for 3 minutes, then immediately transfer them to the boiling broth pot using a spider or slotted spoon. Divide the noodle soup among four bowls and serve immediately.

Knife-Cut Noodles

2½ cups all-purpose flour, plus more for rolling

1 teaspoon kosher salt

2 tablespoons vegetable oil

1 cup water

SERVES 2

Traditionally, Korean knife-cut noodles appear as the base of a soup, or in place of steamed rice as the primary starch accompanying a main dish. The beauty of these all-purpose noodles lies in their imperfection. It's like a bow tie—if it's knotted completely perfectly, it'll look like a corny clip-on. They are noodles made with human hands, not by a pasta machine. Real-deal grandma cooking—not Instagrammable, in the best possible way. This is a base-level recipe that you can take in many directions—a soup with a simple broth, a stir-fry with soy sauce and sesame oil, or even with a spicy chilled noodle dish with Korean Chili Sauce (page 177) and Spicy Ground Pork (page 153). Sub them into "Instant" Ramyun for One (page 102), Black Bean Noodles (page 122), or use in lieu of tofu in the Seafood Stew (page 96). Your keys to success here are a very sharp knife, plenty of extra dusting flour to prevent sticking, and a little patience, as the dough needs to rest an hour before you get busy.

In a stand mixer equipped with a dough hook attachment, combine the flour, salt, oil, and water and mix, starting on slow and gradually increasing speed until fully incorporated. (If you don't have a stand mixer, combine the ingredients in a large bowl and mix them together with a large spoon.) Cover the bowl with a towel, then allow the dough to rest and hydrate for a minimum of 1 hour. Lightly dust a clean work surface with flour. Using a rolling pin, roll the dough out into a large, even rectangular sheet, roughly 15-by-20 inches and ⅛ inch thick, trimming around the edges as necessary. Starting from the bottom, fold the dough sheet away from you and onto itself, section by section, dusting with flour to prevent sticking as needed. Repeat until there are no more folds to make; flip the top lip back onto the fully folded dough sheet if necessary. Use a sharp knife to make small vertical cuts, about the width of linguine, across the surface of the cylinder, from left to right; unspooled, these will form your handmade noodles. Boil the noodles in water for 2 minutes before draining and serving.

Allow the dough to hydrate in a covered bowl for at least 1 hour prior to rolling it out.

Transfer the dough to a clean, lightly floured work surface.

With a rolling pin, roll the dough out into a large, even rectangular sheet, roughly 15-by-20 inches and ⅛ inch thick. Trim the edges as necessary.

Starting from the bottom, fold the dough sheet away from you and onto itself, section by section, dusting with flour to prevent sticking as needed.

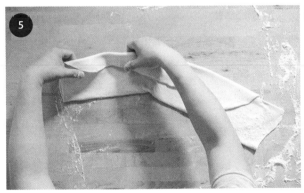

Flip the top lip of the dough sheet back onto the fully folded dough sheet if necessary.

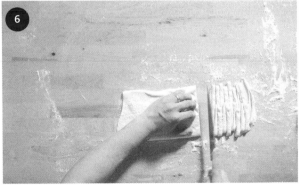

Use a sharp knife to make small vertical cuts, about the width of linguine, across the surface of the fold, from top to bottom; unspooled, these are your handmade noodles.

Black Bean Noodles

½ pound pork shoulder,
cut into chunks

2 tablespoons vegetable oil

4 garlic cloves, sliced

1 tablespoon peeled, minced
ginger

1 large yellow onion, diced

2 tablespoons honey

1 tablespoon kosher salt

1 large carrot, peeled and
cut into 1-inch rounds
(about ½ pound)

½ cup black bean paste

2 cups White Pork Bone Broth
(page 79), chicken stock, or
water

1 large unpeeled Yukon gold
potato, diced

1 zucchini (4 to 6 ounces),
cut into 1-inch rounds,
then quartered

2 pounds fresh udon noodles

SERVES 4

Jajangmyeon has its roots in Chinese cuisine, but it's well-known today as a very Korean preparation. In one of the culture's most sullen yet darkly hilarious traditions, it's the signature dish of April 14, aka "Black Day," a sort of anti-Valentine's when single people dress in gothic attire and drown their romantic woes in mountains of noodles the same color as their clothes, and maybe their souls. Made with black bean paste, the obsidian sauce, typically studded with pork and veggies and twisted into fat noodles, is rich and satisfying; if your teeth turn the color of night, you're doing it right. Regardless of your relationship status, wear an apron while you're cooking and maybe a bib while you're eating—black bean noodle stains are a laundry day nightmare. Also note that this sauce freezes well in plastic storage containers, if you want to have some on hand in the event of a bad breakup.

In a large pot, brown the pork shoulder on all sides in vegetable oil over medium heat for about 5 minutes. Add the garlic, ginger, onion, honey, and salt, stirring occasionally until the onion begins to gain some color, about 10 minutes. Add the carrot, black bean paste, and stock or water, increase heat to high, and boil for 30 minutes. Reduce the heat to low, add the potato and zucchini and cook for 15 minutes more, stirring occasionally, until both are tender. As you're doing this, bring a separate pot of water to a boil and cook the fresh udon noodles for 8 to 10 minutes. Drain the udon, portion the noodles among four bowls, and evenly distribute the sauce over each. Serve immediately.

Chilled Spicy Noodles

4 bundles dried somen noodles

Korean Chili Sauce (page 177) to taste

Quick-Cured Cucumbers (page 32)

Perfect Soft-Boiled Egg (page 48)

1 yellow bell pepper, seeded, cut into small strips

1 large avocado, diced

2 scallions, trimmed and sliced into thin, wispy ribbons (white and light green parts)

1 tablespoon toasted sesame seeds

SERVES 4

This is one of my favorite everyday recipes—Julie makes it constantly throughout the summertime and it's always a hit. It calls for delicate somen, the extruded and dried noodles that take remarkably well to quick-blanching and immediate chilling. While avocado isn't the most Korean touch, it has become a signature addition at my house, as our daughter, Charlie, is still warming up to spice. She'll take one look at the somen here, tossed in my Korean Chili Sauce (page 177), and say, "It's glowing red—super-spicy!" She's absolutely right, of course. The cooling avocado really does help, as do the other veggies and accompaniments called for below; I've been known to "healthy it up" even further by mixing in fresh greens or bean sprouts. Somen is packaged in a variety of quantities, but the noodles are almost always portioned into individual servings of roughly 2 ounces each.

Boil the somen noodles following the package instructions, then cool them down with cold running water. Drain the noodles, then toss them in Korean Chili Sauce to taste. Portion the dressed noodles among four bowls, garnishing with cucumber, soft-boiled egg, bell pepper, avocado, scallions, and toasted sesame seeds. Serve immediately; the dressed noodles will keep in the refrigerator overnight, but not longer.

Somen Noodles with Savory Beef

For the Beef

1 pound lean ground beef

2 tablespoons soy sauce

1 tablespoon sesame oil

1 teaspoon fish sauce

1 tablespoon Dijon mustard

1 tablespoon honey

2 garlic cloves, sliced

½ small yellow onion, diced

1 tablespoon vegetable oil

For the Noodles

4 bundles packaged somen noodles

4 teaspoons soy sauce

2 teaspoons sesame oil

SERVES 4

Here's another somen-centered dish that makes for a crowd-pleasing side dish or lunch. Cold noodles, warm beef—simple and filling. With soy, sesame, fish sauce, and garlic, the marinade for the meat is mostly Korean in style, with a few nontraditional touches (tangy-hot Dijon works so well with beef). Feel free to add any of your favorite vegetables, and/or enjoy with your pick of banchan. Note that the beef should marinate for at least an hour before cooking.

In a large bowl, combine all the ingredients for the beef aside from the vegetable oil, mix well, and allow the beef to marinate, covered in the refrigerator, for 1 to 4 hours. When you're ready, heat the vegetable oil in a large pan over medium-high heat and cook the beef through, about 5 minutes, stirring.

Meanwhile, boil the somen noodles in a medium pot of water following the package instructions, drain them in a colander, and rinse them briefly under cold running water. In another large bowl, dress the noodles with the soy sauce and sesame oil, split them evenly among four bowls, and top with equal portions warm beef.

Sweet Potato Noodles

8 ounces dried sweet potato
noodles

1 tablespoon vegetable oil

2 garlic cloves, sliced

½ small yellow onion, sliced

4 fresh shiitake mushrooms,
sliced

2 medium carrots, peeled and
cut into matchsticks (about
½ cup)

1 scallion, trimmed and cut into
1-inch pieces (white and light
green parts)

1 cup thawed and drained
frozen spinach

1 tablespoon sesame oil

1 teaspoon kosher salt

3 tablespoons soy sauce

1 tablespoon maple syrup

1 teaspoon toasted sesame
seeds

SERVES 4

Much like black bean paste is closely associated with jajangmyeon (page 122) or silken tofu (page 43) evokes instant thoughts of soondubu, sweet potato noodles mean one thing to Koreans, and one thing only: japchae. Frequently made in large quantities for parties and special occasions, it's a communal and celebratory crossover dish everyone seems to enjoy. I think this has a lot to do with the superstar starch. Often sporting a pale, purplish hue, these noodles are remarkably long (have kitchen scissors on hand) and are made from sweet potato flour, giving them a substantial chew that stands up nicely to the double-cooking required here (boiling, then sautéing). This is my rendition of the timeless favorite. It's incidentally vegan, but adding Ground Beef Bulgogi (page 159) is an easy edit for omnivores.

Cook the sweet potato noodles in a large pot of boiling water for about 5 minutes, until they're chewy but not too soft. Drain, rinse under cold running water, use scissors to cut them into 6-inch lengths, and set them aside in a bowl. Heat the oil in a skillet or wok over high heat, add the garlic, onion, mushroom, and carrot, and cook for about 2 minutes, stirring constantly. Add the scallion and stir-fry for an additional minute. Drop the heat to low, incorporate the sweet potato noodles and spinach into the skillet, followed by the sesame oil, salt, soy sauce, and maple syrup. Stir to combine well. Dish out into four bowls immediately, sprinkle with sesame seeds, and serve warm.

Brown Rice

SERVES 4

As essential as white rice is to Korean cuisine, the reality is that it's not the healthiest thing to eat every day. Brown rice is a much more nutritious alternative that can be just as satisfying, as long as you prepare it right. The use of stock, salt, and sesame oil and seeds develops a good base of flavor for this everyday accompaniment. Mix leftover brown rice into soups or stews.

1 teaspoon sesame oil

1 cup long-grain brown rice, rinsed

1½ cups Anchovy Stock (page 78) or chicken stock

1 cup water

¼ teaspoon kosher salt

1 tablespoon white sesame seeds

Heat the sesame oil in a medium saucepan over medium heat. Add the brown rice and toast it until fragrant, shaking the pan occasionally, about 5 minutes. Add stock, water, salt, and sesame seeds, increase heat to bring to a boil, then reduce the heat to low, cover with a small plate, and simmer until the liquid has evaporated, 40 to 45 minutes. Move the pan off-heat, but keep it covered for 10 minutes. Fluff the rice with a fork before serving.

Healthy Rice

SERVES 4

Julie uses our rice cooker to make batches of this alternative rice-and-grain blend that's ideal for everyday meals at our house. She cuts a cup of brown rice with an equal proportion split between lentils and quinoa. It's subtle edits like these, to the pillars of our daily diet, that end up making a huge difference when stretched out across a week, a month, or a year. I enjoy it just as I would conventional white rice, and also incorporate leftovers into soups and stews to make them more nutritious and filling.

1 cup long-grain brown rice

½ cup black, green, or brown dried sprouted lentils

½ cup quinoa

3 cups water

Combine brown rice, lentils, and quinoa in a medium saucepan. Rinse and drain the mixture under cold water, repeating the process several times. Add 3 cups water, then bring the pan to a boil for 5 minutes, stirring occasionally. Reduce the heat to low, cover with the lid, and simmer until the grains are fluffy and the water is fully absorbed, about 30 minutes. Move the pan off-heat but keep it covered for 10 minutes before serving.

Easy Stovetop Rice

1 cup sushi-grade rice

1 cup water

If you don't own a dedicated rice cooker, this is the simplest way to prepare plain white rice to accompany all the dishes in this book. Koreans typically eat standard medium-grain rice at home, but I often spring for the sushi-grade stuff, for no reason other than it's better quality. Rinse your rice thoroughly so the grains separate well when cooking.

Pour the rice into the same pot you plan to cook it in, then rinse and drain it under cold running water several times, until the water runs clear. Add 1 cup water to the pot and bring it to a boil. Reduce the heat to low and cover the pot with a small plate— this will help keep it from boiling over, as it often does with a tighter-fitting lid. After 15 minutes, turn off the heat and allow the rice to rest, covered, for 5 minutes before serving.

Zucchini Rice Porridge

½ cup medium-grain white rice, rinsed

3 cups chicken stock or water

1 medium zucchini, cut in ½-inch half-moons

SERVES 4

Juk, the Korean take on congee usually eaten for breakfast, is the perfect blank canvas for a "clean out the fridge" meal. You can basically incorporate any leftover vegetable, meat, or fish into this porridge. Customize it with a Perfect Hard-Boiled or Perfect Soft-Boiled Egg (page 148), Anything Sauce (page 178), or just plain soy sauce and salt. For this version, I find it tastes best when the zucchini is very soft, with little to no bite to it. I like to serve mine in a large, shallow bowl with a lot of surface area to maximize the amount of additional toppings I can add to it.

Combine the rice and stock or water in a medium pot and boil on high, uncovered and without stirring, until the rice is viscous and the water is about to boil over, about 10 minutes. Reduce the heat to medium, then cook until the porridge has thickened and the rice starts to become suspended in the starch, about 10 minutes more. Stir in the zucchini and cook for an additional 5 minutes, until it becomes soft. Serve immediately.

Spicy Pork Porridge

1 tablespoon sesame oil

¼ pound ground pork

12 pieces pepperoni, chopped

3 garlic cloves, sliced

1½ cups steamed white rice

1 teaspoon kosher salt

1/8 teaspoon Korean chili flake, plus more to taste

3 cups chicken stock, vegetable stock, or Anchovy Stock (page 78)

1 cup frozen vegetable mix (carrots, corn, green beans, peas)

1 cup frozen seafood blend (same used for Seafood Stew, page 96)

SERVES 4

It probably won't surprise you that pepperoni—easily America's most popular pizza topping, from my time at Ledo's until today—doesn't have many applications in traditional Korean cooking. But I took some liberties with this rib-sticking, congee-adjacent dish because it checks so many of our boxes. Pepperoni is available at any grocery store; it's affordable, it keeps for a long time, and (most importantly) it's delicious. The fat rendered from chopped pepperoni, in tandem with the ground pork, creates a robust flavor base. An assertive counterpoint to the Zucchini Rice Porridge (page 130), this recipe is an excellent way to repurpose leftover cooked rice.

In a cold medium saucepan, combine the sesame oil, ground pork, pepperoni, and garlic. Bring the pan to a simmer over medium heat, stirring occasionally, until the fat from the pork and pepperoni has begun to render, about 10 minutes. Stir in the rice, salt, and Korean chili flake, add the stock, and increase the heat to high to bring to a boil, uncovered. Once boiling, reduce the heat to medium to achieve a steady simmer. After 10 minutes, reduce the heat to low and simmer for an additional 8 minutes. Stir in the frozen vegetable mix and frozen seafood blend, cooking until both are thawed and heated through, 3 to 4 minutes. If the porridge gets too thick for your liking during the cooking process, feel free to add additional stock or water. Serve immediately, topped with Perfect Hard-Boiled Eggs (page 48), Perfect Soft-Boiled Eggs (page 48), or Sauna Eggs (page 49).

Ketchup Rice

4 slices (4 ounces) thick-cut bacon, chopped

½ large yellow onion, diced

1 red pepper, seeded and diced

2 small carrots, peeled and cut into ¼-inch coins

2 stalks celery, diced

2 garlic cloves, sliced

½ teaspoon kosher salt

¼ teaspoon black pepper

3 cups Easy Stovetop Rice (page 129)

¼ cup ketchup

4 eggs

Oil or butter for cooking the eggs

Ketchup for serving

2 scallions, trimmed and sliced into thin, wispy ribbons (white and light green parts) for garnish

SERVES 4

Though it originates in Japan, omurice, "omelette rice," is very popular in South Korea in restaurants that specialize in "snack foods." Sometimes it has sausage in it, but I make it with bacon because I like the addition of smoke. My family loves eating this for a weekend lunch and then taking a nap afterwards. Even though I didn't grow up in Japan, there's something nostalgic about ketchup rice, as it's always struck me as something kids enjoy. It's gotta be the ketchup.

In a large nonstick pan, render the bacon for 5 minutes over medium heat. Next, add all your vegetables, salt, and pepper, turn heat to high, and sauté until soft, about 10 minutes. Turn off heat, add steamed rice and ketchup, and mix well. Pack into four medium bowls, then turn these bowls over onto plates. Beat the first of the four eggs and pass it through a fine strainer. In a small nonstick pan with a bit of oil or butter, cook the egg in a thin sheet over low heat, then remove the egg carefully and place it over one of the rice plates. Repeat with the remaining three eggs and rice plates. Finish with a nice zigzag of ketchup and sliced scallion.

Kimchi and Crab Fried Rice

2 tablespoons sesame oil

4 cups cold leftover rice

2 garlic cloves, sliced

½ teaspoon peeled, minced ginger

¾ cup Countertop Kimchi (page 13), drained and chopped

6 ounces picked snow crab meat

1 tablespoon sesame seeds

1 teaspoon Korean chili flake

2 scallions, trimmed and sliced into thin, wispy ribbons (white and light green parts)

1 tablespoon soy sauce

SERVES 4

If the Kimchi and Vegetable Fried Rice (page 142) is a reliable weeknight supper, this Kimchi and Crab Fried Rice is a fancier alternative for a Saturday dinner party. Snow crab is a luxurious add-in with a practical hook: Since it's usually sold already steamed at the supermarket, you don't really have to worry about overcooking it. As with the preceding fried rice methodology, a large, heavy, shallow pan or skillet and cold, day-old rice are imperatives.

Heat the sesame oil over medium heat in a heavy, shallow pan. Add all of the cold rice, breaking it into individual kernels as you introduce it to the pan. Add the garlic and ginger on top of the rice, and let it cook for 3 minutes, without stirring. Stir in the remaining ingredients, cooking for an additional 2 minutes, ensuring everything is well-coated and hot. Serve immediately.

Crispy Mixed Rice

2 chicken legs (about 4 ounces each)

½ teaspoon kosher salt

2 tablespoons sesame oil

1 cup medium-grain white rice, rinsed

1 cup water or chicken stock

2 scallions, trimmed and thinly sliced (white and light green parts)

Korean Chili Sauce (page 177) to taste

For Serving

½ Marinated Spinach recipe (page 42)

½ Marinated Bean Sprouts recipe (page 37)

½ Rolled Omelette recipe (page 50)

SERVES 4

Bibimbap is perhaps the one Korean dish most Americans know by name. Visit any Korean restaurant in the States and there's a high probability they serve it, likely in a dolsot, the screaming-hot stone bowl that's still sizzling when it hits the table. I've always found it funny that it's so famous, because "mixed rice"—what bibimbap literally translates to—is really just that: a bowl of rice with stuff on top. I figure it's gotten so huge here thanks to a combo of the easy-to-grasp format and fun-to-say name. In keeping with that spirit, I'm going to keep my Crispy Mixed Rice simple. I've suggested some of my banchan as additions below, but you can really include or exclude anything you want. It's an excellent way to clear out whatever odds and ends you might have in your fridge before a trip to the grocery store.

Season the chicken legs with the salt. Heat 1 tablespoon of the sesame oil in a medium saucepan over medium heat, and brown the chicken for approximately 5 minutes on each side. Add the rinsed rice and water or stock. Bring to a boil, then reduce the heat to low, cover, and simmer until the liquid is mostly absorbed, about 45 minutes. Turn off the heat and let the pot rest for 10 more minutes without removing the lid. After time's elapsed, remove the chicken legs, pull the meat off the bones, and set it aside. Drizzle the remaining tablespoon of sesame oil over the rice, then cook over medium heat for 10 minutes to brown the bottom-most layer. Scrape the bottom of the pan with a spoon to release the crispy bits, then fold in scallions and Korean Chili Sauce to taste. Serve the rice hot, garnished with the pulled chicken meat, Marinated Spinach, Marinated Bean Sprouts, Rolled Omelette, and whatever other toppings you'd like. Don't forget to mix it up before enjoying.

Mushroom Rice

2 cups (4 ounces) crimini mushrooms, cut into quarters

1½ cups (3 ounces) oyster mushrooms, butts removed, roughly chopped

1 cup (3 ounces) fresh shiitake mushrooms, sliced, stems removed and discarded

2 tablespoons sesame oil

½ teaspoon kosher salt

3 garlic cloves, sliced

1 teaspoon peeled, chopped ginger

1 tablespoon mirin

2 tablespoons soy sauce

1 tablespoon rice wine vinegar

2 tablespoons white sesame seeds

4 cups steamed rice

1 sheet seaweed, cut into fine strips, for garnish

SERVES 4

Back when I was living in New York, I used to go to lunch at a teppanyaki place in the East Village called Robataya. I'd always order the mushroom rice, which could take them 30 minutes or more to make because they did it entirely from scratch, no kitchen tricks or cut corners. It was absolutely worth the short wait, and not just because they gave you pickles and hard-boiled eggs to tide you over while it simmered—it was just one of those perfect dishes that gets stuck in your head like a catchy song, replaying over and over until you get to eat it again. Robataya unfortunately is no longer around, but I've come up with my own version of the mushroom rice. I'd never claim mine is identical, but I like it enough to make for Julie and Charlie regularly. This is the most "restaurant" dish you'll find in this book. The more you cook it, the closer you get to perfecting it. It's simple, but very refined. I think the secret to its appeal lies in the textural experience created by a certain combination of mushrooms, each of which has its own unique qualities that play off the rice itself. I like this dish with a Perfect Soft-Boiled Egg (page 48), though a simple fried egg on top works just as well.

Place all the mushrooms in a cold large sauté pan and add the sesame oil and salt. Turn the heat to medium and allow the mushrooms to steam and release their water. Once the water evaporates, about 10 to 15 minutes, you'll begin browning. Brown the mushrooms for 10 minutes, stirring occasionally. Turn the heat to low, add garlic and ginger, and cook for 3 minutes, stirring occasionally. Add the mirin, soy sauce, rice wine vinegar, sesame seeds, and rice and mix well. Split among four bowls, garnish with seaweed strips, and serve warm.

Kimchi and Vegetable Fried Rice

2 tablespoons sesame oil

4 cups cold leftover rice

2 garlic cloves, sliced

½ teaspoon peeled, minced ginger

2 cups frozen vegetable mix (carrots, corn, green beans, peas)

¾ cup Countertop Kimchi (page 13), chopped and drained

1 tablespoon white sesame seeds

1 teaspoon Korean chili flake

2 scallions, trimmed and sliced into thin, wispy ribbons (white and light green parts)

1 tablespoon soy sauce

2 eggs (optional)

SERVES 4

I developed this fried rice recipe—more of a simple technique, really—after finding myself frustrated with methods that demand too much timing, technique, and specialty equipment from the everyday cook. Yes, I'm a professional chef, but I don't own a wok, and I don't like to cook over super-high heat too often because I live in a rowhouse and I always set off the smoke alarms. The most important aspect of fried rice, for me, is texture—it has to be crispy, but you also have to make sure the rice is seasoned well, and that all the ingredients cook evenly. There are a million methods out there but this is the most straightforward technique I can teach someone to ensure good results. You'll be able to warm and crisp the rice, veggies, and kimchi from the bottom up, while simultaneously steaming the aromatic garlic and ginger without burning it. A large, heavy, shallow pan or skillet and cold, day-old rice are imperatives. My suggestion of frozen vegetable mix is a placeholder; remember that you can incorporate whatever fresh vegetables you have at home into fried rice instead, or in addition.

Heat the sesame oil over medium heat in a large, heavy, shallow pan. Add all of the cold rice, breaking it into individual kernels as you introduce it to the pan. Add the garlic, ginger, and frozen vegetable mix on top of the rice, and let it cook for 3 minutes, without stirring. Stir in all the remaining ingredients (except the eggs), cooking for an additional 2 minutes, ensuring everything is well-coated and hot. If you're adding eggs, scramble them into the rice at this point, or fry separately to place on top. Serve immediately.

Mixed Rice Bites

½ cup frozen vegetable mix (carrots, corn, green beans, peas), thawed and chopped

2 cups warm steamed rice

½ teaspoon soy sauce

1 teaspoon sesame oil

Soy sauce, Korean Chili Sauce (page 177), and crispy seaweed for serving (optional)

SERVES 2

I came up with this recipe for my daughter, Charlie, when I was in charge of packing her lunch every day for preschool. There's no way for the kids to heat anything up, and she's a little too young to be armed with a knife and fork, so it forced me to get a little creative. I steam rice, mix it up with vegetables and meat (if you like), then form it into elongated, bite-size shapes. She could eat them by hand, or with kiddie chopsticks, and we also packed a tiny little cup of soy sauce for dipping. In addition to an easy lunch for your young kids to take with them, this is perfect for a picnic or after-school snack.

Mix all ingredients together in a large bowl, then use your hands to form into tight bite-size portions about the size of your thumb. Make sure you're using warm rice, as the bites will come together and become sturdier as they cool. Serve with additional soy sauce, Korean Chili Sauce, and/or crispy seaweed.

Meat + Grilling

Grilling

Condiments

CONSIDERING THE TREMEN-dous popularity of K-BBQ here in the States, I guess I can understand why some Americans assume that Korean carnivores, from the DMZ down to Jeju-do, spend all their time searing sumptuous short ribs on the luxe smokeless ranges built into their dining room tables. But while Korean barbecue is certainly a beloved format in its country of origin, the preparation of meat, over the kitchen burners or out on the grill, is a much humbler day-to-day discipline for Korean cooks. That's the spirit I'm aiming to capture in this chapter. I love cooking and eating meat dishes just as much as the next chef, but growing into my role as a home cook for my family has really driven home that it's best enjoyed moderately, for nutritional and budgetary reasons alike. While this chapter does feature my recipes for must-haves like BBQ Beef Short Ribs, aka galbi (page 165), and Braised Pork Belly (page 155), I've also included cost-conscious variations on Bulgogi (page 159), a Korea-fied roast chicken (page 149), grillable vegetarian options, versatile condiments, and a number of other nontraditional twists.

Whole BBQ Chicken with Glaze

For the Chicken

1 whole organic chicken, 3 to 4 pounds

Vegetable oil

Kosher salt to taste

For the Glaze

1 teaspoon vegetable oil

2 garlic cloves, sliced

1 tablespoon Korean chili paste

¼ cup mirin

1 teaspoon sesame oil

1 tablespoon white sesame seeds

1 teaspoon soy sauce

1 teaspoon honey

1 tablespoon rice wine vinegar

Steamed rice and banchan of your choosing for serving

SERVES 4 TO 6

This recipe hits all the flavor notes of KFC, Korean Fried Chicken—sweet, salty, spicy, extremely savory. But instead of going through the trouble of setting up a deep fryer or panfrying on the stovetop, which is always a pain and a mess, this is a just-as-delicious recipe for the oven that will impress your family and friends. Please have a lot of napkins handy.

Preheat the oven to 450°F with a rack in the lowest position. Using latex gloves, rub down the chicken with oil and salt to taste, making sure to season inside the carcass, as well. Place the chicken in a shallow baking dish breast side up, tucking the wing tips under the bird so they don't burn. Bake for 1 hour on the bottom oven rack, rotating the bird once halfway through so it browns evenly.

Meanwhile, prepare the glaze. Heat the vegetable oil in a small pot over medium heat, then add the garlic, browning it lightly. Add the remaining glaze ingredients, stirring everything together well, and slowly reduce the glaze by one-third, until it becomes thick enough to coat a spoon.

Once the chicken has baked for 1 hour, remove it from the oven and spoon or brush the glaze all over the bird. Return the chicken to the oven for 5 more minutes, then remove it and allow it to rest for 20 minutes before eating. I like to eat this with white rice and whatever banchan I have on hand.

Roast Pork

3 tablespoons soy sauce

2 garlic cloves, sliced

1 tablespoon sesame oil

1 tablespoon fish sauce

½ cup mirin

1 tablespoon plus 1 teaspoon honey

¼ cup water

1 teaspoon vegetable oil

2 pounds boneless country-style pork ribs

Steamed cabbage, kimchi, and steamed rice for serving

SERVES 4

Country-style pork "ribs" aren't technically ribs—it's a specialty cut from the shoulder that incorporates the meat from the blade and neck sections of the hog. It's an inexpensive but wildly flavorful piece of meat that is often packaged boneless, making it very easy to work with. (Though most butchers will peel off the back membrane from the pork before packaging it, be sure to check and trim it off before cooking if it hasn't been removed.) The braising liquid, featuring soy sauce, fish sauce, mirin, and honey, cooks down into a tangy sweet-and-sour glaze right in the pan, saving you some valuable cooking and dish-washing time. I think it absolutely makes this dish. I recommend serving the pork with steamed cabbage, lettuce wraps, or over steamed rice with kimchi and a fried egg.

Combine all ingredients aside from the vegetable oil and ribs in a small bowl and set aside. Heat the vegetable oil in a medium saucepan over medium heat. Add the ribs, browning them lightly on all sides for about 5 minutes. Remove any excess fat from the pan, then pour the contents of the small bowl over the ribs. Bring to a boil, then reduce the heat to low, cover, and cook for 20 minutes. Flip the pork, then cook for an additional 20 minutes with the lid on. Remove the lid, increase the heat to high and begin reducing the cooking liquid until the ribs start to become sticky and glazed, 8 to 10 minutes—keep an eye on it to make sure it doesn't burn. Slice the pork into large pieces, spooning over some of the pan liquid, and serve with steamed cabbage, kimchi, and steamed rice.

Boiled Country-Style Pork Ribs

1 pound boneless country-style pork ribs

4 cups water

1 serrano chile, scored lengthwise

1 tablespoon kosher salt

1 teaspoon fish sauce

3 tablespoons mirin

1 tablespoon rice wine vinegar

1 tablespoon hot sauce

SERVES 4

This meat lover's preparation of the same country-style pork ribs used for the Roast Pork (page 151) reminds me of an everyday lunch one might enjoy in K-Town. Yes, this isn't the sexiest-looking dish—it's quite literally boiled meat—but I love that the pork, tenderized by the acidic elements of the poaching liquid, has an appealing heat to it, via fresh serrano chile and good old-fashioned hot sauce. Any vinegar-based bottled hot sauce will work well for this recipe; I like to use Red Devil brand.

Add all the ingredients to a large pot. Bring to a boil, then reduce the heat to medium and let simmer, covered, for 1 hour, flipping the pork once after 30 minutes. Let the pork rest on a serving plate for 10 minutes, topping it with a few spoonfuls of its cooking liquid, before serving. Slice the pork into bite-size pieces and serve it with steamed cabbage, steamed rice, Korean Chili Sauce (page 177), Scallion Salad (page 41), and kimchi.

Spicy Ground Pork

1 pound ground pork

1 tablespoon Korean chili paste

1 tablespoon Korean chili flake

1 tablespoon soy sauce

1 tablespoon honey

1 tablespoon sesame oil

1 teaspoon fish sauce

1 teaspoon vegetable oil

1 large yellow onion, sliced

½ teaspoon kosher salt

Lettuce wraps, steamed rice, banchan, and kimchi for serving

SERVES 4

This is a simple recipe for dinner in a rush. I'd recommend marinating the pork covered in the refrigerator overnight, but in a pinch you can combine everything right away and still have solid results. This is the perfect filling for quick lettuce wraps, and also works with Kimchi and Vegetable Fried Rice (page 142), Knife-Cut Noodles (page 120), and Crispy Rice Cakes (page 113).

In a large bowl, combine the ground pork with all ingredients except vegetable oil, onion, and salt and mix everything together well to combine; you can cook it right away, but marinating for at least 1 hour, ideally overnight, is preferable. Once you're ready, combine the vegetable oil, onion, and salt in a large pot over medium heat. Cook, stirring occasionally, until the onion softens and takes on some color, about 5 minutes. Add the marinated pork to the pot, breaking it up with a wooden spoon to ensure it cooks evenly and incorporates with the onions. Cook the meat thoroughly, stirring constantly, about 10 minutes. Serve with lettuce wraps, steamed rice, banchan, and kimchi.

BBQ Pork Belly

½ large yellow onion, sliced

2 garlic cloves, sliced

1 teaspoon vegetable oil

1 pound skin-on pork belly, cut into 2-inch cubes

4 dried shiitake mushrooms, sliced

1 cup water or chicken stock

2 tablespoons light brown sugar

2 tablespoons soy sauce

1 teaspoon fish sauce

1 tablespoon rice wine vinegar

3 cups Napa cabbage (about 5 to 6 leaves), halved lengthwise, then rough-chopped

3 Korean chili peppers, seeded and chopped into large rings

SERVES 4

For this recipe, I drew partial inspiration from twice-cooked pork, a popular dish in Sichuan cuisine. In that preparation, you first boil your pork belly before stir-frying it with leeks, ginger, garlic, spicy peppers, Shaoxing cooking wine, and bean paste. I've got some similar flavors going here—aromatics, fresh Korean chili peppers, rice wine vinegar—but opted for a much less labor-intensive one-pot cooking method. What starts as a sweet-and-salty braise ends as a stir-fry; the cubed pork belly will be tender, but still have a slight, appealing bite to it, a nice contrast to the chopped cabbage and peppers added at the very end. (If you want more heat, don't strip all the seeds from the Korean chili peppers prior to cooking.) I don't usually serve this with anything beyond a side of rice, since there's already so much going on in the bowl.

In a large pot, sweat the onion and garlic in vegetable oil over medium heat. Add the pork belly, plus all remaining ingredients aside from the Napa cabbage and Korean chili peppers, reduce the heat to medium low, cover, and cook for 1½ hours, until the pork belly is tender and a good amount of its fat has been rendered. Add the cabbage and chili peppers and cook for 5 additional minutes, with the lid on, to steam them. Stir everything together before serving.

Braised Pork Belly

2 pounds skin-on pork belly, cut into long, 2- to 3-inch thick strips

3 cups water

Two 12-ounce pilsner beers (I use Budweiser)

5 dried shiitake mushrooms

3 garlic cloves, smashed

2 scallions, trimmed and cut into 2-inch pieces (white and light green parts)

1 tablespoon fish sauce

2 tablespoons soy sauce

1 tablespoon fermented bean paste

¼ cup mirin

1 cinnamon stick

¼ teaspoon ground white pepper

SERVES 4

This is a dish I like to think of as K-BBQ for the home—a way to achieve the same big flavor of an indoor grill without all the smoke and mess. It's also partially inspired by bo ssam (see Note), and can be enjoyed this way, too. The cinnamon and beer in particular create an extremely aromatic end result. When Koreans eat pork belly prepared in this style, they like it to have some bite, with the skin and fat more gelatinous than melt-in-your-mouth tender. Though I recommend slow-braising for 90 minutes, you can let it go for as short as 60 minutes to as long as 2 hours, depending on what consistency you personally like.

Add the pork belly to a large pot, cover with water, and boil for 5 minutes. Remove the pork belly and rinse under cold water, discard the water, and scrub out the pot—this will help remove any funky "barnyard" odors and flavors. Add the pork, the 3 cups fresh water, and all other ingredients to the pot, bring to a boil, then reduce the heat to medium-low and simmer, covered, for 1½ hours (or longer, if you prefer). Slice the pork belly thin and serve it with Korean Chili Sauce (page 177) and steamed Napa cabbage, or use the pork as a topping for "Instant" Ramyun for One (page 102).

NOTE: Bo ssam is traditionally bite-size pieces of pork shoulder or belly, wrapped in lettuce with various condiments and banchan. But the protein can be anything—"ssam" just means "wrapped." I first encountered bo ssam in New York's Koreatown, but it's so adaptable that my family does at-home "ssam nights" all the time. We usually do brisket, Julie's favorite, but it's so easy to swap in another cut of beef, pork, tofu, chicken, roasted vegetables, seafood, and more. Any of the standalone proteins in this chapter can be served ssam-style—just pair it up with lettuce or cabbage wraps, julienned carrot and radish, sliced hot peppers, steamed rice, and my Vegetable Dipping Sauce (page 176), aka ssamjang, to start.

Easy Stovetop Rice (page 129)

Celery Kimchi (page 18)

Braised Pork Belly (page 155)

Ground Beef Bulgogi

1 pound ground beef

½ medium yellow onion, sliced

2 garlic cloves, chopped

2 scallions, trimmed and
cut into 1-inch pieces
(white and light green parts)

1 tablespoon soy sauce

1 tablespoon sesame oil

1 teaspoon kosher salt

1 tablespoon maple syrup

1 teaspoon vegetable oil

SERVES 4

Ground beef gets a bad rap from snobby foodie types, but since it's something I grew up eating, I prefer to see the positive—it's an incredibly affordable and versatile starting point for families looking to save money (aka, all families). It's all about what you do with it. In this recipe, we're using it to prepare a version of bulgogi, one of the most popular dishes in Korean cuisine, both in restaurants and in homes. Typically prepared with fancier cuts of beef, bulgogi rests in a mild, balanced marinade for hours (ideally overnight) before getting crispy and caramelized on the grill. This recipe delivers all that flavor on a hamburger budget. Sweet and salty, it's a flexible base that can be served with lettuce wraps, rice, noodles, or rolled up into homemade Kimbap (page 63).

Combine all ingredients except vegetable oil in a bowl and mix together well. Allow the beef to marinate, covered in the refrigerator, for a minimum of 4 hours, ideally overnight. The next day, heat the vegetable oil in a large sauté pan over medium heat and cook the ground beef thoroughly, stirring occasionally to break up any large chunks. Serve the bulgogi hot, with lettuce or cabbage wraps and steamed rice.

Beef and Tofu Meatballs

1 pound ground beef

¼ pack (roughly 4 ounces) firm tofu, drained and crumbled

½ medium yellow onion, minced

1 medium carrot, peeled and minced (about ¼ cup)

2 scallions, trimmed and sliced (white and light green parts)

2 garlic cloves, minced

1 tablespoon sesame oil

1 teaspoon kosher salt

½ teaspoon freshly ground black pepper

½ cup all-purpose flour

3 eggs, vigorously beaten

2 tablespoons vegetable oil, plus more if necessary, for panfrying

SERVES 4 (MAKES ROUGHLY 20 TO 24 MEATBALLS)

I tend to call these meatballs, but they're really more like meat patties. Working a little firm tofu into your base of ground beef (look for around an 80/20 beef/fat blend) introduces a secondary texture, keeping them soft but not too bouncy. I like to make these for Charlie's lunches because while they taste delicious right out of the pan, they're also good cold and at room temperature. One tip: Be sure to thoroughly beat the eggs to a thin, consistent texture. They won't cling to the meatballs evenly if they're not broken down all the way. Serve with rice, kimchi, and Pancake Dipping Sauce (page 73).

In a large bowl, combine all ingredients except flour, eggs, and vegetable oil and mix well. Make sure the tofu is crumbled into fine pieces so it fully incorporates into the ground beef; this helps bind the "balls" together. Form portions of the beef mixture into small, round patties about the size of a golf ball, collect them on a sheet tray or plate, then smash each down lightly with your palm or a spatula.

Place the flour and beaten eggs into two separate bowls. Add the vegetable oil to a sauté pan over medium heat. Working in modest batches to avoid overcrowding, dredge a handful of meatballs in flour, shake off any excess, then quickly dip each in the beaten eggs before adding them to the hot pan.

Fry each batch of meatballs until cooked though, about 4 minutes per side, transferring them to cool and dry on paper towels. Repeat with the remaining meatballs, adding additional vegetable oil to the pan if necessary.

Grilling

Marinated Skirt Steak

1 pound skirt steak, cut into
4 even pieces

1 medium yellow onion, sliced

4 garlic cloves, sliced

4 scallions, trimmed and
cut into 1-inch pieces
(white and light green parts)

8 dried shiitake mushrooms

2 tablespoons soy sauce

2 tablespoons sesame oil

2 teaspoons kosher salt

4 tablespoons maple syrup

4 tablespoons water

SERVES 4

If you don't have access to Korean-style cross-cut short ribs meant for BBQ Beef Short Ribs, aka galbi (page 165), this is a good alternative that's easy to execute and scratches that steak-night itch. After marinating (overnight is best), grill your meat, inside the kitchen or outside over charcoal, to your preferred temperature, but know that skirt steak is most tender at medium. You can reserve the onions and mushrooms used in the marinade to serve on the side, as well; not only do dried shiitakes boost the flavor of the beef, they absorb marinades in such a way that makes them perfect for grilling or searing. Serve it American-style, with a knife and fork and your favorite sides, or go Korean with lettuce wraps, rice, and banchan such as Potato Salad (page 33) and Scallion Salad (page 41).

Combine all the ingredients in a bowl and mix together well, coating the meat. Transfer everything to a 1-gallon zip-top plastic bag and marinate, refrigerated, for a minimum of 12 hours, ideally overnight. The next day, drain the marinade (reserve it for basting if using a grill rather than a grill pan, see Note). Heat an oiled grill pan over medium-high heat, then add the vegetables and steak. Cook the steaks for 2 minutes per side, and allow them to rest for 4 to 5 minutes before slicing them against the grain. Remove the vegetables once they are nicely caramelized. You can also prepare this dish on an outdoor grill using indirect heat (see Note). Eat with lettuce wraps, steamed rice, Korean Chili Sauce (page 177), and your pick of banchan.

recipe continues ⟶

A Note on Grilling

If you're using gas, simply turn one side on high and leave the other side off to achieve indirect heat. If you're using a conventional charcoal grill, use a chimney to ignite your coals, then arrange them all on one side of the grill, leaving the other side empty. When the lid is closed on either type of grill, you want a temperature at or around 400°F. Before cooking, clean the grill with a brush, then use a paper towel and tongs to apply a light layer of oil to the grate. Start your food on direct heat with the lid off, flipping frequently as needed; this will develop a good char before you transfer it to indirect heat and cook to your desired temperature (lid on, if the recipe calls for it). Remember that with meats like skirt steak and short ribs, the indirect heat cooking time will be very quick, since they're thin, flat cuts; recipes like the oyster mushrooms will take longer.

BBQ Beef Short Ribs

2 pounds Korean-style beef short ribs, cross-cut, 1 inch thick

½ cup soy sauce

¼ cup light brown sugar, packed

1 large Asian pear, peeled and chopped

3 garlic cloves

1 tablespoon mirin

1 tablespoon sesame oil

1 tablespoon peeled, chopped ginger

½ medium yellow onion, chopped

1 tablespoon vegetable oil, plus more for grilling

SERVES 4

I understand that this wouldn't be a Korean cookbook without a recipe for galbi, or grilled marinated short ribs, but I'll admit that for the longest time, I preferred to buy the meat already marinated from a place like H Mart. It took me trying many restaurant versions, which I often find too sugary, and just as many at-home recipes—Julie's mother's, most memorably—for me to home in on the exact levels of salty, sweet, and savory for the home cook. I'm very happy with this version and any cookout you grace with these ribs will be happy, too. I fully expect and encourage you to customize this marinade to your liking once you're familiar with it. No matter how you tweak, however, leave the Asian pear alone, as the natural enzymes in the fruit help tenderize the beef. Note the same exact marinade works in vegetarian/vegan applications for tofu and mushrooms, too.

Rinse the short ribs with cold water and be sure to remove any bone shards. Place all ingredients aside from the beef in a blender and puree until smooth. Combine the beef and the puree in a 1-gallon zip-top plastic bag or large sealable container and marinate for 24 to 48 hours. Remove the short ribs from the marinade (discard the marinade) and pat off any excess liquid with a paper towel. Rub the ribs lightly with additional vegetable oil and grill them over indirect heat (see Note, page 164) for 10 minutes. The beef should be well done, as the marinade will keep it moist and tender. Serve with steamed rice and banchan.

Broccoli Kimchi (page 23)

Easy Stovetop Rice (page 129)

Potato Salad (page 33)

Pickled Daikon Radish (page 40)

Quick-Cured Cucumbers (page 32)

BBQ Beef Short Ribs (page 165)

Marinated Spinach (page 42)

Pickled Daikon Radish (page 40)

BBQ King Oyster Mushrooms (page 171)

Roasted Cauliflower

3 tablespoons Korean chili paste

2 tablespoons fermented bean paste

2 tablespoons rice wine vinegar

2 tablespoons mirin

2 tablespoons raw sugar

1 tablespoon soy sauce

1 tablespoon sesame oil

1 head cauliflower, trimmed of leaves, bottom sliced flat, and halved lengthwise

SERVES 4

At backyard cookouts, I always empathize with people who don't eat meat. They're surrounded by salivating carnivores, but when the big moment comes and the grillmaster pulls some perfectly mid-rare masterpiece off the flames, they're stuck with chips and pasta salad. This is one for them—a barbecue-friendly main dish that's grill-ready, but can also be prepared in the oven to accompany everything sizzling outside. Though this is a very nontraditional recipe, the sweet-and-spicy marinade (vegan, too) delivers plenty of balanced Korean flavor to the cauliflower, which turns tender after roasting, while still retaining some of that veggie crunch. You can present it whole, and even carve it tableside to add a little "wow" factor before serving it ssam-style.

Whisk all ingredients except the cauliflower in a mixing bowl to make a marinade. Transfer to a 1-gallon zip-top plastic bag, add the cauliflower halves, and refrigerate for 24 hours. Preheat the oven to 375°F. Add ½ cup of water to the bottom of an oven-safe roasting pan, then transfer the marinated cauliflower to the center of the pan, reserving any excess marinade. Roast the cauliflower for 30 minutes, then remove it from the oven and use a brush or spoon to baste it with the reserved marinade. Add another ½ cup of water to the bottom of the pan, turn the cauliflower then roast it for an additional 30 minutes. Allow the cauliflower to rest for 15 minutes before slicing it and serving it warm with lettuce wraps and steamed rice.

If you're using a grill (see Note, page 164): Grill the cauliflower halves over indirect heat, about 15 minutes per side. Flip each half as needed to prevent burning (about three times should do it). Brush reserved marinade evenly on both halves with

recipe continues ⟶

each turn. Keep the grill lid closed when you're not brushing or flipping; this will essentially also bake and smoke the cauliflower while it grills. When finished, it should be nicely charred all over and tender when pierced with the tip of a knife. Transfer the cauliflower to a serving platter and allow it to rest for 15 minutes before serving.

BBQ King Oyster Mushrooms

3 tablespoons soy sauce

1 tablespoons sesame oil

2 tablespoons maple syrup

1 tablespoon Dijon mustard

2 garlic cloves, sliced

1 tablespoon mirin

1 tablespoon rice wine vinegar

1 tablespoon fermented bean paste

1 tablespoon water

1 pound king oyster mushrooms, cut in half lengthwise

SERVES 4

Substantial and sturdy, king oysters take on marinades and a smoky char incredibly well, making them the ideal vegan/vegetarian option for a cookout. It's a mushroom that's just meant to be grilled, largely because it doesn't cook so differently from a piece of meat. Using Dijon mustard provides that horseradish/wasabi-style spice and thickens the marinade for better basting. These mushrooms can be the primary focus of a cookout plate, and leftovers are an appealing addition to soups, stews, Kimbap (page 63), and more.

Whisk all ingredients except the mushrooms in a bowl. Collect the mushrooms in a 1-gallon zip-top plastic bag, pour in the contents of the bowl, and marinate at room temperature for 4 hours, or in the refrigerator for 12 to 24 hours. Reserve the marinade for basting. Grill (see Note, page 164) over direct heat for 2 minutes per side, then shift to indirect heat for 20 minutes with the grill lid closed, basting the mushrooms with the leftover marinade during grilling. If you don't want to cook over gas or charcoal, use a grill pan, sauté pan, or roast in the oven at 400°F to get color. Serve hot, cold, or room temperature, with steamed rice, as banchan, or cut up as an addition to a soup or stew.

Quick-Cured Cucumbers (page 32)

Marinated Mushrooms (page 38)

Easy Stovetop Rice (page 129)

Spicy Shrimp Skewers

1 pound 16 to 20 count shrimp, about 20 pieces, peeled and deveined

3 tablespoons Korean chili paste

¼ cup sugar

Juice of ½ lemon (about 1 tablespoon)

2 garlic cloves, minced

1 teaspoon peeled, minced ginger

1 scallion, trimmed and thinly sliced (white and light green parts)

1 tablespoon white sesame seeds

1 red bell pepper, seeded, cut into large chunks

1 large sweet onion, cut into large chunks

SERVES 4

This is a nice dish for a warm night when you feel like firing up the grill: a simple, healthy shrimp skewer that is slightly spicy and delicious. The vegetables stay crunchy and light and the shrimp keep their nice bite. Make sure you use sweet onions for this recipe, so the onions don't need to be cooked through. Serve with steamed rice, Healthy Rice (page 128), and your banchan of your choosing. I recommend Quick-Cured Cucumbers (page 32) and Pickled Iceberg Lettuce (page 39).

Combine all ingredients except bell pepper and onion in a 1-gallon zip-top plastic bag and allow the shrimp to marinate for about 30 minutes in the refrigerator. Reserve the marinade. Using four wooden or metal skewers (soak them for 30 minutes pre-grilling if using wood), prepare kebabs of shrimp, green pepper, and sweet onion, alternating, until you have four to five shrimp per skewer. Prepare a grill for direct cooking over high heat. Grill the skewers over direct heat for 2 minutes. Brush excess marinade over shrimp, and grill on the other side for 2 more minutes. Serve hot.

Condiments

Black Pepper Oil

1 tablespoon freshly cracked
black peppercorns

4 tablespoons vegetable oil

MAKES 4 TABLESPOONS

Any recipe that calls for black pepper, either as an ingredient or an after-the-fact seasoning, can be improved by swapping in this infused oil instead. I use heat to extract the natural fruitiness of peppercorns, which is often lost when you're cracking it on top of your food. Drizzle this oil over your favorite rice, noodles, dumplings, or soup; it can also be incorporated directly into recipes like Soy-Braised Beef (page 64), Oxtail Vegetable Stew (page 90), Oxtail Soup (page 92), and Korean Army Stew (page 94).

Heat pepper and oil together in a small pan over medium heat until the pepper starts to "fry," about 3 minutes. Cut off heat and allow the pepper to infuse into the oil as it cools, about 10 minutes more. Store the oil with the pepper at room temperature.

Vegetable Dipping Sauce

¼ cup fermented bean paste

2 tablespoons Korean chili paste

2 tablespoons sesame oil

1 tablespoon honey

2 teaspoons sesame seeds

1 garlic clove, minced

½ small yellow onion, diced

SERVES 8 AS A CONDIMENT

This is my rendition of the traditional condiment known as ssamjang. At Korean barbecue places, it's served as a dipping sauce for raw vegetables like cucumbers, peppers, and carrots, as well as a spicy accompaniment for grilled meats. Julie enjoys ssamjang best when it's fresh, which means there's always some left over after a meal, since there are only three of us enjoying it. Luckily, it keeps for quite a while, and every time I make another batch I get to taste newer and older versions of the same sauce side by side. It's a similar philosophy to kimchi, in that it's enlightening to try the same recipe in different stages and see how it develops. Typically, the up-front spice will mellow over time, and the savory umami flavors will deepen.

Combine all ingredients in a medium bowl and mix well. Serve at room temperature. Refrigerate in an airtight container for up to 2 weeks.

Korean Chili Sauce

½ cup Korean chili paste

1 garlic clove, minced

2 teaspoons sesame oil

1 tablespoon honey

1 tablespoon maple syrup

1 tablespoon apple cider vinegar

2 tablespoons water

1 tablespoon white sesame seeds

SERVES 4

This is a Korean "master sauce" that I love to use for rice cakes, mixed rice dishes, over noodles, and more. If everything's incorporated correctly, it'll be thick and plenty spicy. Too hot? Hit it with a little honey, maple syrup, or sugar to temper it down, if needed. This differs from the preceding Vegetable Dipping Sauce (page 176), or ssamjang, in that hot Korean chili paste, not plain fermented bean paste, is the base of flavor; the addition of maple syrup, vinegar, and water makes for a thinner, leaner spicy sauce.

Combine all ingredients in a medium bowl and mix well. Refrigerate in an airtight container for up to 2 weeks.

Anything Sauce

2 tablespoons soy sauce

1 tablespoon sesame oil

¼ teaspoon peeled, chopped ginger

3 scallions, trimmed and thinly sliced (white and light green parts)

1 tablespoon vegetable oil

MAKES ¾ CUP FRESH, ½ CUP AFTER MARINATING

For my money, this might be the most versatile homemade condiment you can keep in your fridge—a true "anything" sauce. Toss Knife-Cut Noodles (page 120) with it, use it to top Zucchini Rice Porridge (page 130) or plain old rice (page 129); or go off-grid and use it on your eggs for breakfast, or like gravy on your mashed potatoes. Add a bit of Korean chili flake if you want it spicier.

Combine all ingredients in a medium bowl and mix well. Refrigerate in an airtight container for up to 2 weeks.

Potato Chip Chili Crunch

½ cup crushed kettle-cooked salt and vinegar potato chips (go for a gravel-like consistency)

¼ cup canola oil

1 tablespoon sesame oil

1 tablespoon roasted sesame seeds

1 teaspoon onion powder

½ teaspoon garlic powder

½ teaspoon paprika

½ teaspoon kosher salt

½ teaspoon granulated sugar

¼ teaspoon ground coriander

¼ teaspoon ground white pepper

MAKES ABOUT 1 CUP

When it comes to homemade condiments, I value versatility—it's the best way to encourage us to actually use and enjoy what we make. Much like my Anything Sauce (page 178), this nontraditional riff on the ever-popular chili crisp works on, well, anything: eggs, soups, stews, noodles, and more. A no-cook recipe, it's remarkably easy to throw together and the "secret" ingredient is something you can purchase anywhere: salt and vinegar potato chips. It delivers the addictive texture chili crisp fanatics crave—go for a kettle-cooked brand to maximize crunch—and the salt and vinegar flavoring fires up the taste buds. I went conservative on spice to start, as Charlie doesn't do mega-hot just yet, but it's easy to customize by working in Korean chili flake, or even crushed Calabrian chilies. Avoid incorporating anything with high water content, like bottled hot sauce, as it'll detract from the crunch factor.

Combine all ingredients in a small bowl and mix together well. This can be served straight away, but I recommend letting it sit refrigerated in a covered container for 1 to 2 days to allow all the flavors to infuse into the oil. Mix the condiment together well before enjoying, as the solids will sink to the bottom over time. It will keep in the refrigerator in a covered container for 1 week.

Desserts + Drinks

Stuffed Fried Bread

For the Fried Bread

1 cup all-purpose flour, plus 2 tablespoons for working dough

½ teaspoon kosher salt

1 teaspoon granulated sugar

1 teaspoon instant dry yeast

½ cup lukewarm milk

2 tablespoons neutral oil for cooking

For the Filling

⅓ cup light brown sugar

½ teaspoon ground cinnamon

1 tablespoon maple syrup

¼ cup unsweetened shredded coconut

Pinch kosher salt

SERVES 4

Hoetteok is a common Korean street food: a thin griddled dough round with savory fillings, like cheese, or a stuffing of noodles and vegetables. Looking something like the beautiful love child of a flapjack, a quesadilla, and an English muffin, it's one of the most beloved snacks in the country. There are sweet versions, too, so that's what I'm running with here. I developed this recipe for Charlie, and in a way it reminds me of the cinnamon-sugar toast I'd make for myself as a kid when there was nothing sweet in the house. I like my hoetteok warm, fresh out of the pan, but you can also enjoy them at room temperature.

Combine all fried bread ingredients except the oil in a large bowl, mix them together well, and cover with a towel. Leave the dough to rise for 1 to 2 hours, until it doubles in size.

Shortly before you're ready to cook, combine all filling ingredients in a small bowl and mix well.

Using scissors, cut the dough ball into quarters; each portion should be around the size of a golf ball. Lightly flour your hands, then gently stretch the dough into small, even, pancake shapes, roughly 4 inches across. Place one-quarter of the filling in the middle of each uncooked dough round, then bring the edges together evenly to cover the filling, pinching it closed. Cook each fried bread in oil in a nonstick pan over medium heat, 2 to 3 minutes per side until browned, gently pressing down with a spatula after flipping. You should only need to flip them once if you are cooking them at the right temperature.

Poached Asian Pears

2 cups white wine (a sweeter style works well)

1 cup brown sugar

1 cup maple syrup

1 cinnamon stick

2 chamomile tea bags

1 teaspoon peeled, chopped ginger

4 large Asian pears, peeled (reserve peels), quartered, seeds removed

SERVES 4

I really like to eat these elegant poached pears on their own, though they do make a fancy accompaniment for a nice piece of cake or scoop of ice cream. They're good warm, cold, or room temperature, in large part because Asian pears have the integrity to hold their juiciness and texture even after a long cooking process. The secret weapon of this recipe is flowery chamomile tea, which I've always felt works so well in Asian-style desserts, as well as being a foil for brown sugar. It might seem like there's a ton of sugar in this recipe, but remember that the oven-poaching process provides nice flavor and texture without leaving the fruit cloyingly sweet.

Preheat the oven to 275°F. In a large, oven-safe pot, bring all the ingredients except the pears (but including their peels) to a boil. Add the pears to the liquid, transfer to the oven, and bake, uncovered, for 1½ hours, turning the pears twice during the process. The fruit should be cooked, but still have bite. Serve warm, or cool in their strained cooking liquid and serve at room temperature. You may also chill them and serve them cold.

Cinnamon-Sugar Rice Cakes

½ of the Crispy Rice Cakes recipe, before boiling and pan-searing (page 113)

1½ cups sugar

1 tablespoon plus 1 teaspoon ground cinnamon

2 teaspoons ground ginger

½ teaspoon kosher salt

SERVES 4

This is not a classic Korean dessert. Usually, you'd find rice cakes stuffed with sweet bean paste, but I developed this preparation as a shoutout to my childhood love of all things cinnamon-sugar (see Stuffed Fried Bread, page 183). These are simple and delicious, and my daughter loves them for their chewy texture.

Cut the rice cakes into small balls, about the size of a donut hole. Combine the remaining ingredients in a bowl and set aside. Bring a medium pot of water to a boil, reduce to a steady simmer, then poach the rice cakes for about 10 minutes. Remove the cakes with a slotted spoon and drain well before gently transferring them to the cinnamon-sugar bowl. Toss the poached rice cakes with the mixture to coat them evenly, and allow them to cool slightly before serving.

Jujube Tea

15 dried jujubes

6 cups water

¼ teaspoon peeled, chopped ginger

1 cinnamon stick

3 tablespoons honey

SERVES 4

You can find the jujube fruit at most Asian supermarkets, but since their fresh season lasts only about a month in the early fall, they're usually sold dried. They have all sorts of purported health benefits, from improved digestion to helping with sleep, but I really just love this tea, known as daechucha in Korea, because it's incredibly light and refreshing over ice in the summertime. I'd describe jujube fruit's flavor as somewhere in between a date and an apple, with a crisp, dry finish.

Bring all ingredients except honey to a boil in a medium pot. Turn off heat, cover, and allow the tea to steep for 15 minutes. Strain out solids and add the honey to finish. Enjoy warm or cold.

Korean Yogurt Drink

One 5-ounce container plain Greek yogurt

1 cup unflavored rice milk (I used Rice Dream)

Juice of ½ a lemon

2 tablespoons honey

Ice for serving (optional)

NOTE: I use Greek yogurt with strawberry on the bottom. It makes this drink pink, sweeter, and "on brand."

SERVES 1

This is, hands down, Charlie's favorite recipe—I'd make it for her after she got home from pre-K, and before long she started requesting that I bring it for her in a mason jar so she could enjoy it on the walk back. She loves the classic packaged Korean yogurt drinks, but I don't like that they're packed with stuff like high fructose corn syrup or aspartame. My version is pretty dead-on, down to the creamy cumulus cloud-like color.

Puree all ingredients in a blender until smooth, about 1 minute. Serve over ice, if using.

Chocolate Rice Pudding

½ cup heavy cream

1½ cups milk

½ cup sweetened condensed milk

1 teaspoon vanilla extract

2 tablespoons sugar

2 tablespoons cocoa powder

1 cup steamed rice

2 tablespoons semisweet chocolate chips, chopped

SERVES 4

This is a streamlined version of a slightly cheffier dessert we did at Pete's Place. It's a nice way to turn the leftover rice you always seem to have around into something unexpectedly delicious—whether the rice is warm or cold, it'll work great. This is also something you can pre-prepare as many as 4 days in advance and keep in your refrigerator, to save time for an upcoming dinner party. In addition to the chocolate chips, feel free to finish it off with fresh chopped fruit or whipped cream.

Preheat the oven to 300°F. In a medium, oven-safe saucepan, combine heavy cream, ½ cup of the milk, condensed milk, and vanilla extract and bring to a boil, stirring occasionally. Stir in sugar and cocoa powder until fully incorporated, then mix in the steamed rice thoroughly. Transfer saucepan to the preheated oven and bake, uncovered, for 1 hour. Allow the pudding to cool completely, then stir in the remaining 1 cup milk to thin it out. Garnish with chopped chocolate chips before serving.

Honey Butter Rice

2 tablespoons butter, melted

2 tablespoons honey

2 cups warm Easy Stovetop Rice (page 129)

1 ginger tea bag

3 tablespoons warm water

2 teaspoons vegetable oil

2 tablespoons powdered sugar

SERVES 4

Here's a quick, rice-based sweet treat that isn't a rice pudding. It's an excellent way to use leftover rice. Charlie loves the combination of crunchy and chewy you achieve here by crisping up warm, tea-infused rice in a pan. I like using ginger tea because it complements the honey butter topping well, but feel free to substitute chamomile tea, or any other flavor you'd like. Just be careful not to use a caffeinated tea if you're making this for kids.

Mix together the melted butter and honey in a small dish and set aside. In a bowl, combine the warm rice and the contents of the ginger tea bag and mix well, incorporating the warm water to help the tea infuse into the rice. Heat the oil in a large nonstick pan over medium heat, then add the tea-infused rice, pressing it out evenly to form a pancake shape roughly the circumference of the pan. Cook the rice until browned and crispy, 4 to 5 minutes a side, then transfer to a serving plate. Slice into four wedges, drizzle the honey-butter evenly over the wedges, then finish with a dusting of powdered sugar passed through a fine mesh sieve. Eat immediately.

Acknowledgments

I would like to thank my mom and dad, Sally and Dennis Serpico, for always supporting me and pushing me to grow. My brother, Danny, for always being the voice of reason and the best roommate growing up. My sisters, Terra and Jackie, for being the best sisters and always having my back. My wife, Julie, for being the glue that holds our family together. My daughter, Charlie, who brings me the greatest joy. My friends Quino, Chino, and Yao, for the ability to have long phone conversations out of the blue. Stephen Starr and STARR Restaurants, for taking a chance on me. Dave Chang, for being a big brother and mentor. Drew Lazor, Rica Allenic, and W. W. Norton, for making this cookbook a reality. Neal Santos, Ed Newton, Geri Radin, and Brian Croney, for capturing the beautiful photos in my home during the global pandemic. Bonnie and Tim Miller, for always treating me like their third son growing up. Michele and Russ Gledhill, for the summers at the beach. Brian Giniewski, for handmaking the beautiful dishes in this book. Great Jones, for the beautiful cookware. Anyday, for the amazing microwave cookware. To all the chefs, GMs, cooks, writers, purveyors, farmers, dishwashers, cooks, bartenders, hosts, and servers that I've worked with along the way: thank you all for being a part of my journey.

Index

Note: Page references in *italics* indicate photographs.